Production Design

Production Design: Visual Design for Film and Television is a hands-on guide to the craft of Production Design and Art Direction. Author Peg McClellan gives an insider's view of the experiences and challenges of working as a Production Designer in film and television.

The book covers three major areas, starting with an overview and the basics of job responsibilities, the artistic approach and the background which every Production Designer needs to be familiar with, and progressing to the mechanics of the role with a day-to-day breakdown of the job itself. McClellan takes you through script analysis, team collaborations, the hierarchy of a production, hiring a team, the business elements, locations, studio facilities, handling change, and everything in between.

With case studies, insights from successful Production Designers, and inspiration in the form of over 200 colour photos and illustrations from storyboards to sets, this is the ideal book for students seeking a career in production design, and professionals looking to further their design knowledge.

Peg McClellan is an Emmy Award-winning Illustrator and Production Designer; she has worked on feature films such as *Seabiscuit*, *Brokedown Palace*, and *Coal Miner's Daughter*, plus several television series, including *Melrose Place* and *CSI*. She is an instructor in Production Design at the Academy of Art University in San Francisco and also teaches a course in Visual Design for Film at Dodge Film School, Chapman University, Orange, California.

Production Design

Visual Design for Film and Television

Peg McClellan

Routledge
Taylor & Francis Group

LONDON AND NEW YORK

First published 2020
by Routledge
52 Vanderbilt Avenue, New York, NY 10017

and by Routledge
2 Park Square, Milton Park, Abingdon, Oxon, OX14 4RN

Routledge is an imprint of the Taylor & Francis Group, an informa business

© 2020 Taylor & Francis

Library of Congress Cataloging-in-Publication Data
A catalog record for this title has been requested

ISBN: 978-1-138-18543-2 (hbk)
ISBN: 978-1-138-18542-5 (pbk)
ISBN: 978-1-315-64452-3 (ebk)

Typeset in Frutiger and Palatino
by Servis Filmsetting Ltd, Stockport, Cheshire

Contents

What Is Production Design?

What is Production Design, anyway? Does anybody know?

—Jimmy Kimmel, host, Academy Awards 2017

The title of Production Designer was *created* as a *special title* for Art Director **Wm. Cameron Menzies** on Gone With the Wind, because Menzies famously did so much more than Art Direction on that film.

For example, he designed, storyboarded and filmed the burning of Atlanta scene—which was inspired when he heard about the studio planning to tear down part of their backlot buildings and build new.

His countless illustrations, construction drawings, and set designs included costumes and set dressing, impeccably researched. He was involved in nearly every meeting on the film.

Because of his extraordinary involvement on the film, when it was nominated for Best Picture Award, Mr. Selznick wanted to create a new and special category, above and beyond Art Direction. This is where the title Production Designer comes from.

In order to define who should get an Oscar for Production Design, the Academy of Motion Pictures Arts and Sciences has defined the Production Designer as the person who is PRIMARILY RESPONSIBLE for the design of the production and the execution of that concept, as verified by the producer.

There was a time when the majority of the principle or lead designers on movies or TV shows were given the title *Art Director*. My contemporaries and I did the work of Production Designers, but our resumes and IMDb listings show us as Art Directors on our early projects. The title of Production Designer is more ubiquitous now and Art Directors today are seen as associates of Production Designers on productions.

—Norm Newberry (Six Million Dollar Man, Mask, Gotcha!)

The title of Production Design is meant to be *earned*.

There is no Production Design official occupational code. Legally, we are all Art Directors.

—Chuck Parker, Executive Director Art Directors Guild, Local #800

00.01 WM Cameron
Menzies & Lyle Wheeler

00.02 Art Director Al Nozaki
with early model of spaceship he
designed for *War of the Worlds*

The Production Designer is <u>**the head of the Art Department**</u> on any project. The platform may be a documentary, a commercial, a music video, a television show, web series, a feature film, or theatre—the job of the Production Designer is the same on every project.

Every Production Designer has their own style, and every project is different.

This book is meant to be a guidebook, to help navigate the job of Production Design, showing the day-to-day mechanics, the necessary skills, and the responsibilities.

The tools we use will change, as the rapidly revolutionizing tech field has already shown. Even as this book is being written and published, there will be new tech developments which will date those we use today.

Technology is simply another tool in the Production Designer's toolbox, not by any means the most important.

No matter how the tools and platforms change, GOOD DESIGN WILL ALWAYS BE A NECESSARY REQUIREMENT.

00.03 *Hooded Falcon*, 1924 (never made). Courtesy of the Menzies family collection

Production Design is the total control of the visual aspects of cinematic presentation; complete.

Whatever is happening visually on the screen, that's Production Design.

Production Design is 'indefinable'; the position knows no bounds.

Computers will never replace us because they cannot VISUALIZE or CONCEPTUALIZE.

—Rick Carter (Star Wars, Lincoln, Forrest Gump, Avatar)

I'm not sure you can teach Production Design, because you have to know too much.

—Jim Bissell (Mission Impossible, Good Night, Good Luck, Monuments Men)

Where he stands, is he in motion, coat on or off, texture, color, size, shape, the workings of it—<u>that</u> is Production Design.

—John Decuir, Sr.

CHAPTER 1

The Language of Visuals

Good Production Design is best if it isn't noticed at all …

Production Design is trying to figure out what goes on the screen visually to determine 'the look' of the project.

— Tom Duffield (Production Designer, *Lone Survivor, Patriots Day, Hell or High Water, Ed Wood*)

As a Production Designer, you need to be able to discern **what is most important** to put on the screen, how much to spend on it, and how to showcase it, so that *you determine what the viewer will remember **in an instant***.

Your design has to 'read' quickly and give **all** of the information necessary. The ability to accomplish this is possibly the most important skill in great Production Design. It's based on instinct, awareness, and experience. Additionally, a great Production Designer knows **how** to prioritize the visual images **without any dialogue**.

One of the best and most valuable skills I have learned in my film business training, both as an Illustrator and as a Production Designer, was *how to focus on what is important*.

Where do we put the money? Where do we want the audience to look?

Directing the visuals from this approach takes time and experience to learn. It's the visual equivalent **of determining the 'broad strokes' before the details**. Beginners and amateurs usually focus too early on the details. This wastes time and is pointless because once the major concepts are resolved, *the details take care of themselves. In other words, discipline yourself to **EDIT**. Use only the **best, most appropriate visuals** in the project*.

Simplify.

A well-designed set should support the story and reveal/define the character(s). Similar to actors, Production Designers **interpret** the story, **interpret** the Director's vision, and **interpret** each character. The use of visual 'clues' should read like a treasure map, instantly defining the style, economic status, gender, hobbies, and interests—even geographical locale—of each character and setting. Every design decision should support the story and the character. It is the actor's equivalent of '***building a backstory***' for the character.

Figure 1.1 *The Son of the Sheik* (Valentino), 1926, courtesy of the Menzies family collection (cover design)

Figure 1.2 *The Son of the Sheik*, 1926, courtesy of the Menzies family collection

The Art of Production Design

Art is in the head! The tools don't matter, the ideas are what count.
— Nelson Coates (Flight, Runaway Jury, 50 Shades Darker, Flight,
Kiss the Girls)

Production Designer as a job title means **the head of the Art Department** on any project. The platform may be a documentary, a commercial, a music video, a television show, web series, a feature film, or theatre—the job of the Production Designer is the same on every project.

Every Production Designer has their own style, and every project is different.

The tools we use will change, as the rapidly revolutionizing tech field has already shown. Even as this book is being written and published, there will be new tech developments that will date those mentioned here. The point is, technology is simply another tool in the Production Designer's toolbox, not by any means the most important, just the most current.

No matter how the tools and platforms change, ART AND VISION are irreplaceable. *The idea, telling the story, bringing imagination, dreams and emotions to life are what artists do.*

It's the musician, dreaming the original tune in their head, where nothing yet exists. It's the painter, imagining the portrait in colours before the model appears. It's the writer, feeling something so strongly that it needs to come out of thin air into the light—GOOD DESIGN WILL ALWAYS BE A NECESSARY REQUIREMENT.

Figure 1.3 *The Hooded Falcon*, 1924, never made, courtesy of the Menzies family collection

Design is the realization of vision.

The *approach* to designing or finding the look is always the same, no matter the project: You search, research, and **open your mind and senses** to anything and everything you can find that may be pertinent to your project. And then—often when you are not looking for it—you find that one perfect image that is absolutely right on every level.

When this happens, you just *know* it's right.

Often, the off-times are when inspiration occurs. Learn to trust this inspiration! Don't overthink this part of the job, because it is more than just facts; it involves emotions. This phase should be fun and creative; it's why Production Design is called an **art.**

Every project is different. Every challenge is different. But the process remains the same. You immerse yourself in the written world (the story or **script**), your Director communicates their **emotional point of view** (their **vision**), and *your job is to marry the two appropriately.* Then you allow the magic to happen—the magic of designing **the look**, the magic that is **the power of visuals**.

The Production Designer's Role

The Production Designer is the head of the Art Department. In addition to the Production Designer, the Art Department consists of an **Art Director**, **Set Designers**

Figure 1.5 Stage set, *She*, 1935. Designed by Art Director Van Nest Polglase, the 'ancient' temple where Queen Hash-A-Mo-Tep dwells doesn't look so spectacular from this angle, but the entourage of actors, crew, and visitors on the set of the adventure/fantasy *She* makes for an impressive array of humanity on set.

Figure 1.6 Collaboration of PD Henry Bumstead and Alfred Hitchcock

Bummy (left) looking over plans for Vertigo with Hitchcock, production manager C. O. "Doc" Erickson (second from left), and associate producer Herbert Coleman (right). Courtesy of Henry Bumstead.

(i.e. draftsmen), **Illustrators** (sketch artists for concept sketches, production sketches, and storyboards), **Graphic Designers** (for signage, logos, etc.), an **Art Department Coordinator**, and an **Assistant Art Director**.

Production design is not self-indulgent; no job is ever the same, and will never have the same approach. In fact, the less the set design is noticed, the more successful it is. Make it **believable, authentic, and real**.

The Production Designer oversees the work of the **Costume Designer, Hair and Make-Up,** and the **Props and Set-Decorating** Departments. Because ALL elements of a project will have design considerations, the Production Designer also oversees occasional stunts and special effects.

Figure 1.7 Van Nest Polglase/RKO

The Script

There <u>must</u> be a story to tell. You don't design a set, you design a picture first, <u>then</u> you design a set.
—Dick Sylbert (*The Graduate, Baby Doll, Chinatown, Rosemary's* Baby, Dick *Tracy*)

You need to know literature—<u>this is a storytelling job</u>!
—Jeannine Oppewall (*LA Confidential, Pleasantville, Catch Me If You Can, Seabiscuit*)

Good Production Design always supports the character and the story above all else. Production design is <u>the craft of giving visual clues to the audience</u>. Nothing should be designed before the characters and the story are understood.

The Production Designer first reads the script to **visualize an approach to the design that will support the story and characters** in terms of colour, texture, light, composition, movement, time period, and locale.

It's always what's right for the story; what's the ESSENTIAL thing. It will not always be size. It can be line, form, color—how any of these affects the sets *emotionally*. Menzies knew the premise. *He knew where he was going.*
—John DeCuir, Sr (*Cleopatra, Hello Dolly, The King and I*)

We need to create a back story for each character, so that every surface tells a story … the audience will sense all the backstory! You just have to *feel* it.
—Wynn Thomas (*Hidden Figures, A Beautiful Mind, Inside Man, Do The Right Thing*)

The script becomes your journal and blueprint for the project.

Your script should become your personal catalogue containing all the notes and details pertaining to the project. Label it and always carry it with you!

Alfred Hitchcock famously said—'You need three documents to make a movie: a budget, a schedule and a script. You shoot them in that order.'

In reality, 'Hitch' thought that the script was the most important thing (along with a full set of storyboards for the entire movie). Those were the tools that were the guides for his crews, and 'woe be to anyone who didn't abide by them!'

Never assume someone else will have a script; always be prepared and always have your script with you! It will contain page changes, up-to-date Director's notes, quick sketches, location details, possibly even camera set ups. Your script will be so personalized, it will be a true record of the entire project—even quotations!

<u>THE SET BECOMES THE CHARACTER</u>

Hitchcock believed that 'we need to make distinct environments' for each of the characters, such as 'one character always drives the red car, or another character lives in a brick apartment building, so always use brick when that character is seen—it helps the audience'.
> —Henry Bumstead (Production Designer, *The Sting, To Kill a Mockingbird, Vertigo*)

As Production Designer, you are making the characters come to life through every visual decision you make. It's fun, once you get started and everyone is on board. It's like acting, in a way, only you are performing using architecture instead of dialogue.

We need to create a back story for each character, so that every surface tells a story … the audience will sense all the backstory! You just have to feel it.
> —Wynn Thomas (*Hidden Figures, A Beautiful Mind, Inside Man, Do The Right Thing*)

Imagination

When reading a script for the first time, you will automatically envision and begin to imagine a 'look' for the show, based on the writer's descriptions. Designing in a way that *supports your characters* takes some serious thought and focus, because once established, this approach becomes the **design brief** for the entire show. You begin to **have fun** looking for ways to support your theme with subtle yet strongly visual choices.

Your design approach should be approved by your Director. 'No surprises!' is the motto of Production Designer Tom Duffield. Always keep the Director informed.

The Director will consider your input and ideas based on their own vision of the story and who the characters are. It's important that the two of you are in agreement. Hopefully, the Director will appreciate the depth and focus you bring to a simple office or bedroom set. Once you are in sync with the Director, they can better direct and block the actors within the sets you've created.

Your design brief becomes a blueprint for everyone on the show, including Set Decorator, Prop Master, and Cinematographer, as well as wardrobe and hair and make-up. The design brief is often delivered in a verbal discussion supplemented with visual materials posted on large boards, but can also be delivered in a document.

Each department needs a direction for the design approach; it's up to you, as Production Designer, to give it to them (after it's been approved by the Director, of course). This direction makes everyone's job easier. Soon, there will be times when a department head will find you to say, 'Just wait until you see what we found for this character!'

When this occurs, you will know that a team effort is in place.

The television series *Downton Abbey* is an example of excellent Production Design with meticulous attention to detail that supports the story and characters. In *Downton Abbey*, the location needed to convey tradition, social order, symmetry, quality, wealth, history, heritage, and grandeur, all while providing a home for families, both upstairs and downstairs. The design is all in service to the characters. In fact, through the lush design and its pervasive presence in every episode, the manor house becomes more than a place to live; it is a character itself.

Figure 1.8 *Downton Abbey* set model

As a set, the colour palette upstairs is warm, for the family. Downstairs, for the servants, the colours are all neutrals. Each character's room provides clues to her or his nature. These details are deliberate, not accidental or random. If a character is strong and rugged, the furnishings reflect athletics and adventure; if the character is artistic, original drawings, paintings, books, and art supplies are evident. All are clues to the character who lives there; nothing is accidental. Every choice is deliberate, thought out, and approved by the creator, Julian Fellowes, and the Director, both of whom have the overall vision of every character firmly in their minds.

These basics give the audience clues to the characters. Often, a good set will help the actors to step into their characters and their own personal worlds.

> We have to think like an actor; we are storytellers; we give experiences.
> —Jim Bissell (*ET, Mission Impossible—Rogue Nation, Monuments Men, Good Night, and Good Luck*)

What Is Appropriate

Production design is not self-indulgent; it should never be the same, and never have a noticeable 'style'. In fact, the less the set design is noticed, the more successful it is. Make it **believable, authentic, and real**.

It is exciting and good for your own design growth to be challenged in each script by new sets to design and new characters to interpret. Designing, building, and striking sets within a week or less opens up opportunities most designers outside of the entertainment industry never have.

Figure 1.9 PD Dick Sylbert on set

Look for clues to your characters before you design anything. Once you have your approach, or plan (known as a 'design brief'), everything falls into place. Decisions become easy, because if something doesn't fit the character, you know you must find a better option.

Production Designer Richard (Dick) Sylbert was a literary man, and would **search for a theme** to his projects before designing anything or even selecting locations. On *Chinatown*, for example, the theme was water and drought, so his *design decisions were all based on the theme of water symbolizing wealth*. The only character who had any living greenery, growing plants, or lush lawns was the richest man in town, because he could afford to pay for water. To push the point, the production went over-the-top with an entire greenhouse of orchids! Everyone else in the story had dry lawns, brown dirt, and dead trees.

The lush visual impact of living plants, fragile orchids is an example of Production Design creating the appropriate emotion for the character, the story, and for the scene.

Story and Character 1

It's critical to remember to resist the temptation of designing for design's sake. Here is a great example:

Academy Award-winning Art Director, Henry Bumstead, liked to tell the story of the first set he was allowed to design for a show on his own:

> the script called for an apartment, so I drew plans for the set to be built using *rich crown moldings, lots of paneling, and walls and walls of bookshelves* (his dream apartment).
>
> When the Supervisor, Hans Drier ('a very *learned* man'), walked in to view the result, he walked through the entire set in silence.
>
> He then said, 'Very nice apartment … **obviously, the character is well-read and affluent; what does he do for a living?'**
>
> The Art Director answered, 'Well, *the script says he is a plumber.'*
>
> The Supervisor left without a word.

The next day, 'Bummy' (as he was known in the industry) **revised his set** to reflect *one that a plumber would live in*: **a set to support the character**, not his own design aesthetic.

Bummy liked to tell this story to make the point that Production Design is **not about the Designer's personal tastes**; it *has to serve both the story and the character.*

From then on, Bummy built a reputation for the **authenticity of his sets**, which brought him two Academy Awards and multiple nominations (*To Kill a Mockingbird*, *The Sting*).

Clint Eastwood's first choice for Production Designer on most of his films was Bummy, in part because his sets were so believable and authentic.

Two examples: Bummy built a Boston bar set for the movie *Mystic River* and a boxing ring set for *Million Dollar Baby*. Both looked so realistic that tourists often wanted to visit these locations! Of course, they didn't exist anymore; they were just sets that had to be struck after production ended.

Figure 1.10 Interior bar set, *Mystic River*

Collaboration

Although I can do everybody's job, I need them to achieve my vision.
                                                    —James Cameron (Director)

A collaborative nature is definitely a strength; recognize the need for others.
        —Rick Carter (*Star Wars, Lincoln, Forrest Gump, Avatar, Star Wars, Jurassic Park*)

Traditionally, it is the **Director**, the **Production Designer**, and the **Cinematographer** (or Director of Photography), who form a **triumvirate** that creates *the visual style* of the project. These roles complement one another, and collaboration is crucial to the project's success. *A successful collaboration with the* Cinematographer *can literally make or break your sets and 'the look'.*

It is imperative that this important relationship be cultivated immediately during pre-production; the Cinematographer will bring ideas and suggestions to the project that will improve and affect your sets and jump-start the design. These ideas affect the Set Decorating Department as well, especially when it comes to windows (with blinds, curtains, and/or or shutters) and practical lighting.

The Director is the Captain of your ship; it's his film, and the only reason we're there is for whatever visual and dramatic things we can add to his picture.

I can't say enough about the need for the team to be together!

You all need to stay <u>close</u>. Because it's in that closeness where the opportunity for achievement rests.

                                —John DeCuir, Sr (*Cleopatra, Hello Dolly, The King and I*)

Figure 1.11 Filmmaking triumvirate. (a) Digital illustration. (b) Digital illustration of the 'Director's vision', with notes.

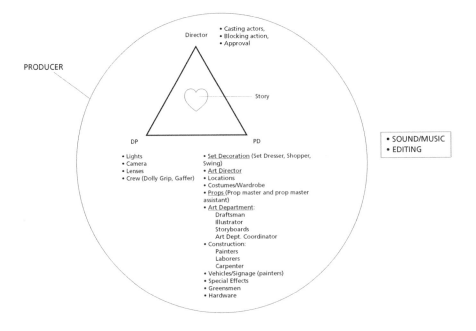

Figure 1.11 Continued

Director's Vision
–Numbered script
1 Theme
2 Colour Palette
3 Emotional Tone

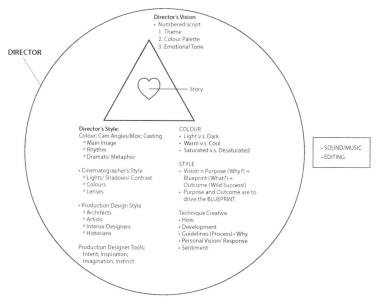

COLOUR
• Light v.s. Dark
• Warm v.s. Cool
• Saturated v.s. Desaturated

STYLE
• Vision = Purpose (Why?) + Blueprint (What?) + Outcome (Wild Success!)
• Purpose and Outcome are to drive the BLUEPRINT

Technique	Creative
• How	• Why
• Development	• Personal Vision/ Response
• Guidelines (Process)	• Sentiment

• Director's Style:
Colour: Cam Angles/Mov; Casting
—> Main Image
—> Rhythm
—> Dramatic Metaphor

• Cinematographer's Style
—> Lights/ Shadows/ Contrast
—> Colours
—> Lenses

• Production Design Style
—> Architects
—> Artists
—> Interior Designers
—> Historians
Production Designer Tools: Intent; Inspiration; Imagination; Instinct

Your design brief becomes a blueprint for everyone on the show, including Set Decorator, Prop Master, and Cinematographer, as well as wardrobe and hair and make-up. As we have mentioned, the design brief is often delivered in a verbal discussion supplemented with visual materials posted on large boards, but can also be delivered in a document. Each department needs a direction for the design approach; it's up to you, as Production Designer, to give it to them (after it's been approved by the Director, of course).

This direction makes everyone's job easier. Soon, there will be times when a department head will find you to say, 'Just wait until you see what we found for this character!' When this occurs, you will know that a team effort is in place.

As Production Designer, you are making the characters come to life through every visual decision you make. And it's fun, once you get started and everyone is on board. It's like acting, in a way, only you are performing using architecture instead of dialogue.

What it is is 'getting your arms around this thing and sticking everybody in that box including the cameraman and making the picture that is completely unified; WHOLE.

Just like a good piece of music or a good painting. A good painting isn't good in one corner, it's good all over the place.

A good piece of music isn't good in the middle, it's good everywhere and it ALWAYS connects, always.

This note affects that note. this becomes a theme if you put these notes together.

It has a different color here and a different tempo here but it is one piece of music and that's the real *fun*.'

—Dick Sylbert (*The Graduate, Baby Doll, Chinatown, Rosemary's Baby, Dick Tracy*)

You're like the leader of the orchestra; you don't have to know how to PLAY every instrument well, but it's your responsibility to know how to make each of them come together and make something beautiful.

—Rick Carter (*Star Wars, Lincoln, Forrest Gump, Avatar, Jurassic Park*)

Translating Words into Pictures

by Peter Wooley (*Blazing Saddles*)

Do you realize that every time you read a book without pictures you become a Production Designer, Casting Director, Costume Designer, even the Cinematographer? Hell, you can be a Director if you want to.

Whether you know it or not, when you read a book without pictures, your brain fills in the blank spots. You can see the people, how they are dressed, which way they are moving, and what it looks like around them. Neat, huh?

Well, this is what I've been doing for the last forty years; reading scripts, and translating those words into pictures. I let my brain hum along with the words, and I draw what I 'see.'

When I design a set I'm going to build on a stage, I let the words guide me. (Thank you, writers everywhere.) By the time I am finished 'realizing' the set, its looks spill out of the end of my pencil, I give the sketches to my design and construction team. Days, weeks or months later, viola, a physical manifestation of what I had in my head. We light it, act in it, and photograph it.

Then it's torn down—or 'struck'—as we say, and the stage is bare for another designer's vision.

(Some day I'll tell you how I learned to do this sitting on my grandparents' living room floor listening to the radio.) God bless radio.

Did I mention they pay me to do this?

CHAPTER 2

The Business of Production Design

You have to please the people with the money, because without the money, nothing moves. Give them an <u>honest</u> budget. You have to level. It takes a lot of talking; you have to be right in there with the Director and the Producer.

There's a big difference between a Production Manager who just pinches the pennies and the Production Manager who watches the pennies <u>and</u> who wants to make a fine film.

—John DeCuir, Sr (*Cleopatra, Hello Dolly, The King and I*)

This chapter will explain how to break down a script into industry-standard segments; you will learn how to judge the 'weight' of a script, meaning how many pages are Interior (INT) vs Exterior (EXT), DAY vs NIGHT, and SETS vs LOCATIONS. You will also become familiar with creating a budget, which, aside from your script, will be the single most important document you'll need on any project.

John DeCuir, Sr was a talented artist and a great showman; he believed that 'bigger is always better' when pitching visuals for a project.

He approached his projects with an eye for the grand scale (*Cleopatra* almost bankrupted its production studio, and the *Hello Dolly* street still stands on the twentieth-century backlot).

DeCuir had very high standards, and he naturally 'thought big' … as a result, he earned the reputation of an 'expensive designer'—one who would cost the production money—yet his multiple Academy Award nominations proved the value of good Production Design and offset this reputation with positive **box office returns**.

Years ago, when working on a concept presentation for the Epcot Center (then a new venture), with his son, John DeCuir, Jr, he designed a 'virtual reality' ride … a new concept at the time.

For the presentation meetings in Florida, he insisted on making the design renderings oversized (3' {x} 4', instead of the standard 28" {x} 36").

John knew that the team they were presenting to were expecting something 'really big' from Hollywood designers … he didn't stop at size; he wanted the <u>number</u> of renderings for the pitch to be <u>more</u> than the usual 3 or 4. He *doubled* the number of oversized renderings, which cost them <u>twice the price</u>.

John DeCuir, Sr's mantra was: 'WE HAVE TO WOW THEM!!! OTHERWISE, WHAT'S THE POINT?'

Know where to put the money!
—Jim Bissell (*ET, Mission Impossible—Rogue Nation, Monuments Men, Good Night and Good Luck*)

Knowing where to put the money is one of the most important skills of a Production Designer; it can make all the difference between a memorable scene and one that's forgettable—

You have to think about the budget always … find an approach that's 'simple as possible'; <u>reduce</u>, simple is <u>best</u>.
—Jeannine Oppewal (*LA Confidential, Pleasantville, Catch Me If You Can, Seabiscuit*)

I treat the budget like Congress; the House and Senate come up with budgets and present to the President (Producer).
—Tom Duffield (*Lone Survivor, Patriots Day, Hell or High Water, Ed Wood*)

Be a part of the conversation when money is allocated and spent. Most people are working with money issues; restrictions don't scare me. We still have to figure out a way to make the project.
—Wynn Thomas (*Hidden Figures, A Beautiful Mind, Inside Man, Do The Right Thing*)

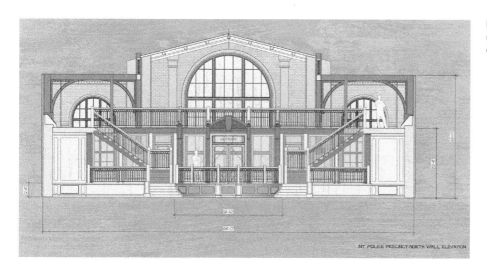

Figure 2.0 *Gotham* computer rendering/ elevation sketch

Figure 2.1 *Gotham* computer rendering

Figure 2.1 *Gotham* computer rendering

The Script

> The thing is to tell the story as *succinctly* and *easily* as possible.
> —Bob Boyle (*North By Northwest, Cape Fear, Thomas Crown Affair, The Birds*)

Before you can design anything, you receive a script to read. This becomes the primary resource (sometimes referred to as the 'bible') for all of your ideas, because within the script pages are design parameters, requirements, boundaries, and specifics that you are being invited to create and develop.

Enjoy this first read; try to resist making notes. Your mind will be racing, full of ideas and questions. This is the exciting part—right now, anything is possible, because there is no budget, no reality of locations vs builds, cast, crew, or calendar and, most importantly, no Director's point of view. These will follow soon enough.

> Read the script, scribble your first impressions in the script, just little studies, or stick figures; the important thing is that the information is noted.
> —John DeCuir, Sr (*Cleopatra, Hello Dolly, The King and I*)

> Sometimes there isn't a finished script, so try to find the biggest problem in those pages you have and resolve them completely with the Director. The biggest problems are always the ones that plague you if you put them aside.
> —Ted Haworth (*Strangers on a Train, Some Like It Hot, Longest Day, Marty*)

When you meet with the Director, he or she will want to hear your ideas. **Be prepared!** Show the Director visuals whenever possible—artwork, colours, landscapes—but don't be too specific; *convey a tone.* Try to tackle the biggest, most important sets and scenes, or the most difficult ones. Surely, these will be uppermost in the Director's mind, too, and you will show foresight and anticipation by attempting to bring clarity to any difficult scenarios.

> Prioritize the sets; there are always 2 or 3 main ones you really put effort on.
> —Henry Bumstead (*The Sting, To Kill a Mockingbird, Vertigo*)

The Director has had the script longer than you, and has had time to work on it. Chances are that she or he has some very clear ideas about what to show and how to shoot it. This is good! This is when you **listen** and become a master communicator by interpreting the Director's ideas. Find out what is important to him/her. The ability to translate these ideas to your approach for the sets and locations is the heart of good Production Design.

Production design is not self-indulgent; it must interpret the Director's point of view and support the story at all times.

> It's not about <u>your</u> taste, it's about <u>the character's taste</u>!
> —Nelson Coates (*Runaway Jury, 50 Shades Darker, Flight, Kiss the Girls*)

Design must also start with the business end, which is a budget. There are three questions every creative needs to ask when considering a job or a project:

1. What is the **scope of work**?
2. What is the **time frame**?
3. What is the **budget**?

Approaching every project with these three questions informs your decisions intelligently and realistically. For example, if the production requires you to build a temple, and it's needed tomorrow, it will be a rush job requiring a large 24-hour crew, which will cost a lot more money!

One Production Manager *at Disney had a plaque made for his office, which read: 'FAST, CHEAP, GOOD. Pick two'.* The formula works; you can never have all three!

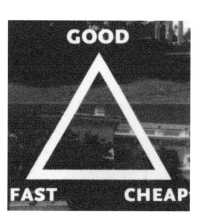

Figure 2.2 Triangle: fast, good, cheap

> Budget isn't first, ideas are first! Art is in the head! It doesn't matter what the tools are, the ideas are what count. Draw, sketch, draft—push yourself to know what you need to know how to do the job; know the language.
>
> —Nelson Coates (*Runaway Jury, 50 Shades Darker, Flight, Kiss the Girls*)

Armed with an idea of the Director's vision and knowing how much time you have to shoot the project, you can begin to 'break down the script', which simply means **organizing the details and prioritizing**.

In television, you usually begin with a **pilot** script—the first of the new series. (A series order is typically for between six and thirteen episodes.) The pilot may be a bit longer than a typical episode (one hour for a half-hour show or two hours for a one-hour show), with a budget to match. These initial sets will set the tone for future episodes and establish the characters and the locale. Sets will be **permanent sets** (main), **swing sets** (occasionally used, so they 'swing' on and off stage), or **locations**.

You will receive the script for the next episode **while you are shooting the current show**. Often, the Director will change with every new episode (your crew remains the same throughout). So now you are juggling two scripts, two Directors, and two shooting schedules, plus the occasional insert or re-shoot from the previous show.

Clearly, series television is one of the most challenging jobs in the business.

You must be fast. The need for speed and organization cannot be overstated. With 5–7 days per script, your sets are conceived, designed and drawn, built, painted, dressed, and ready to shoot within a few days; after sets are shot they're 'struck' (usually the following day, to make room for the next … and on and on). To **strike** means to tear down or remove. Production is a moving train, and your job is to stay ahead of it.

The good news: *your growth as a Production Designer will be HUGE.* Because you run through so many different scenarios so quickly, your expertise in creating offices, restaurants, police stations, hospitals, etc. becomes almost shorthand, and you will find yourself wanting to 'push the boundaries' of the norm. This is when some **really** interesting design occurs.

Script Breakdown

Make your own script breakdown. The Art Director's breakdown sheet should contain the **set title,** whether it's to be an **interior or an exterior** setting, **day and/or night**, **scene numbers**, and **page count**.

Each set, whether it's a building or a practical location, is given a **set number**.

Very few scripts are sent out without set numbers. (When, and if they are, script numbers are usually negotiated with the Accounting Department. These days the preference is for 3-digit numbers for their accounting programs. If someone numbers a script on their own, there is a good likelihood that all of those numbers will be changed if Accounting and the Assistant Directors haven't been consulted.)

Additional items to include (for cost-accounting purposes when figuring the budget) would be **special effects**, **signage**, **graphics**, **greens**, **backings**, and, of course, **strike** (including the cost of labour and materials to strike a set or location and restore it to its original condition before filming).

CGI, or computer graphics, may or may not come out of your budget; this is something to bring up with your Production Manager immediately. If you are paying for it, you are responsible for the look of it. Otherwise, it may be contracted to an outside company (vendor) with its own art direction team. This may present a problem with consistency of the visual style and require your diplomatic skills and clarity with all involved.

"BACKDOORS"

SAN FRANCISCO LOCATIONS

SCENES	NO	SET TITLE	D/N	LOC	PGS
1-19		INT-EXT CABLE CAR	D/	HYDE ST.	3
20-27	–	EXT. TURNTABLE & BARN	N		2
28-29		INT. POLICE BLDG. CORR	N	S.F. HALL of JUST.	1¼
30-31	–	INT. CORONERS AREA	N		3¼
32	–	EXT. S.F. STREETS (BELLS SEQ.)	D		¼
58-60		INT. POLICE GARAGE	D	S.F. HALL of JUST	1
67-69		EXT. RICO'S STALL	D	FISHERMANS WHARF	2
70-71		EXT. COOPER BLDG	D	S.F. ALCOA BLDG	½
166-174, 85, 78, 126, 147-155, 231	–	INT. POLICE SQUAD RM.	D&N	S.F. HALL of JUST	10
80-84		INT.-EXT TRENCH'S HOTEL & LOBBY	D	CHESTNUT ST.	4
86-93	–	EXT. RAINIES APT. & FOYER	D	3RD ST?	1¾
122-125	–	EXT. BOAT SLIP	D	SAUSALITO	4
127-129		EXT. S.F. STREET (HAROLD BUSTED)	D		1
130-133		EXT. S.F. ALLEY (FRIEND BUSTED)	N		½
140-146	–	INT. PROPERTY ROOM	D	S.F. HALL OF JUST	3
156-165	–	EXT. OLD GUN EMPLACEMENT	D	SAUSALITIO	4
175	–	EXT. PHONE BOOTH	N		⅛
179-206		EXT. S.F. STREET & ROOFTOP	DUSK?		4
226-230	–	EXT. McBRIDE'S HOUSE	N		7
241-243	–	EXT. S.F. STREET (McBRIDE TAIL)	D		¾
244-247		EXT. BASEMENT RESTAURANT	D		1
251-303		INT-EXT WHARF & WAREHOUSES	D	PIER 47	8½
					63

The first breakdowns are going to be subject to a lot of revisions. Before going to a hard copy, stay flexible with draft copies that group sets and locations by type, locale, or time period.

Figure 2.3 Early script breakdown (Ward Preston)

Hell or High Water Prelim. Set List (undated draft) 3/28/15

Set No.	Set	D/N	Location	Backings	Greens	Construction	Total
001	Archer City Prairie	D					
002	Ext. First Texas Bank - Archer City, TX	D					
003	Int. First Texas Bank - Archer City, TX	D					
004	Int. 1988 Camaro (Driving)	D					
005	Ext. Two Lane Hwy - Camaro	D					
006	Int. First Texas Bank - Olney,TX	D					
007	Ext. First Texas Bank - Olney,TX	D					
008	Int. Texas Rangers Office - Abilene,TX	D					
009	Ext. Hanson Ranch	D/Sunset/N					
010	Int. Hanson Ranch House-Liv Rm,B.R., Kitchen	D/N					
011	Int. Diner - Vernon (across from 'other' Bank)	D/N					
012	Int. West Texas'other' Bank - Vernon,TX	D/N					
013	Ext. Diner - Vernon, TX	Late PM					
014	Int. Taurus - Vernon,TX	D					
015	Int. Lincoln - Marcus/Brushfire	D/Sunset					
016	Ext. Country Road - Lincoln	D/Sunset					
017	Int. Chevy Blazer/dirt road/bump gate	N/D					
018	Ext. Tanner's Trailer	N					
019	Int. Tanner's Trailer	N					
020	Ext. Gas Station	N					
021	Ext. Commanche Red River Casino	N					
022	Int. Commanche Red River Casino & Front Desk Bar, Chip Window, Poker Tbl, Hotel Room	N					
023	Int. Best Western Motel Room - Vernon,TX	N/Dawn					
024	Ext. Best Western Motel Room - Vernon,TX	N/Dawn					
025	Ext. Used Car Lot - Lawton, OK	Dawn					
026	Int. T-Bones Cafe - Coleman,TX	D					
027	Ext. T-Bones Cafe - Coleman,TX	D/N					
028	Int. Debbie's House - Childress,TX	D					
029	Ext. Debbie's House - Back Porch - Childress,TX	D					
030	Int. Rayburn Law Office - Seymour,TX	D					
031	Ext. Texas Highway	Dawn					
032	Ext. First Texas Bank - Jayton (Closed)	D					
033	Ext. Highway 380 - below 'Caprock', near Post	D					
035	Ext. Main Street - Post, TX	D					
036	Int. First Texas Bank - Post, TX	D					
037	Int. Grand Am - Pos, TX	D					
038	Ext. Gran Am - Hwy 380 - Tanner gears up	D					
039	Ext. Hilltop - Oak Tree - Tanner Last Stand	D					
040	Ext. Ridge Line - Marcus targets Tanner	D					
041	Int. Indian Casino -Check In & Toby's Room	N					
042	Int. First Texas Bank - Childress, TX - Loans	D					
043	Ext. Marcus' House - Abilene, TX	D					
044	Int. Marcus' House - Abilene, TX	D					
			TOTALS				

Figure 2.4 Set list breakdown form: *Hell or High Water*

For example, computer graphic images that appear on screen may need to be generated by an outside contractor (also known as a **vendor**). **You**, the Production Designer, know the shooting schedule for that scene and when the images need to be delivered. The Production Designer is also aware of the colour palette, the Director's vision, and the purpose of the graphic images, duration on screen, etc. This is why the Production Designer should be involved with the creation of all aspects of these images.

Even if these images aren't included in your budget, you can see how important it is that your vision is taken into consideration when creating them. It is essential to make time to meet with any outside contractors (i.e. vendors), and whenever possible, schedule a preview with the Director for approval of these images during pre-production.

Remember to include phantom sets in your budget. **Phantom sets** are images you see on a show or in a movie that sometimes appear on electronic screens. They include monitor images and could appear in a script (e.g. EXT SCENE OF AN ACCIDENT). These may require set construction and can therefore impact the budget significantly.

Here are some additional considerations:

- **Photos** mentioned in the story: pre-production work may be required to get still photos of the actors (with backgrounds!) to be used as props or additional set dressing.
- Some **continuous shots** may require more than one location.

> To me, the most interesting thing about Production Design is that every picture has its own problems.
>
> —Bob Boyle (*North by Northwest, Cape Fear, Thomas Crown Affair, The Birds*)

Breakdown and Budgeting (Part 1)

Each detail written in your script deserves your attention, not just for the look, but from a cost, scheduling, and production standpoint; your marked-up script will become your 'bible'. Use coloured inks for different departments, margin notes, highlighters—whatever you feel comfortable with—but *make your script your own and keep it with you at all times.*

Page counts help you determine the *number of actual sets* and *locations* the script requires, which helps determine the budget. Industry standard is the **1/8-page method**, in which you basically divide each page (*the text*) into eighths. This indicates the amount of shooting that's scripted for each set.

Breaking Down a Script

First, you are given a script. See if it has numbered scenes. If not, you will need to number the scenes.

Breakdown Form

Next, using your numbered script, fill out your blank breakdown form (also called a **set list** form).

Figure 2.5 Set list

Your Name:

Title of the Production:

Set List

Scene #	Set #	Int/Ext	Description	Day/Night	Page Count

Scene 1 will be Set 1: EXT SAN FRANCISCO SKYLINE—DAY

Let's examine the columns and how you'd fill them in for this scene:

- The first column is the Scene Number (1)
- Second column is the Set Number (1)
- Third column is INT/EXT—choose one (EXT)
- Fourth column is the Description (San Francisco Skyline)
  - It's okay to abbreviate the description 1/8
- Fifth column is Day/Night—choose one (D)
- Sixth column is Stage/Location (Location)
  - In this column, you choose whether the scene will be filmed on location or on a sound stage
- The seventh and final column is Page Count, which is the number of eighths of a page of a scene (1/8)
  - This is the *length* of the scene, **not the page number the scene is on**.

Our first scene is 1/8 of a page in length. The convention in the film business is to use eighths of pages. (You do not need to reduce the fractions, unless it's a whole number.) This convention is used to estimate the length of every scene.

Determining Scene Length/Page Count/Eighths

Start by assuming every script page has eight eighths (8/8) of text.

Every scene will be some number of eighths. Using the lines you drew across the top of every slugline/scene heading as a guide, look at the length of each scene on the page. By looking at the space between the lines you drew, you can estimate how many eighths of a page should be indicated for each scene.

Decide how many eighths comprise each scene, and write the number down in the margin of the script, as in the examples. When you have gone through the whole page in this way, count your measurements to make sure the page has a total of eight eighths. If you end up with only 6/8ths or 9/8ths, for example, you'll need to readjust your measurements.

Once you have done this for the entire script, you will be able to add the page counts of scenes that take place on the same set. *Knowing the total page count for every set will be essential for your work in the production*.

In addition, lengthy scenes may require storyboards to break down the action, and page counts are a good way to determine when this need exists.

Breakdown and Budgeting (Part 2)

At the beginning of a set list, you may have a one-to-one correspondence with the set and scene numbers. As you continue further into a script, you'll see that this correspondence won't last forever.

Note: When you're breaking down an entire script and creating the breakdown form (a.k.a. set list), you may want to use index cards to list each set, as well as the scenes that take place on the set. This will help you to decide the *importance of a set* when you're budgeting and scheduling. When figuring out the length of a scene, remember that the scene may continue to the next page or even go on for a few pages; your page count could get lengthy.

Ultimately, when you're doing separate Production Design breakdown sheets for all the sets in a film, the information on the breakdown form/set list is used. You will count up the pages for a given set (for each scene that takes place on the set), and that gives you the total page count for the set. (The index cards help with this, too.)

Figure 2.6 1/8-page method

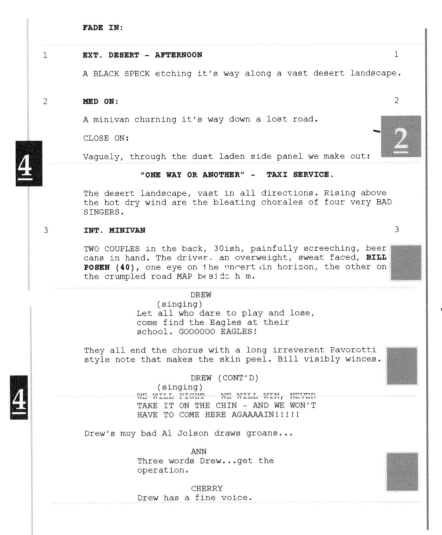

Measuring the scenes in this way is a **fundamental concept that underlies the functioning of the entire production. It is also critical to your budget, because you need to know the page count for each scene you break down in the script**. Page count helps determine whether a set should be a location or build, because the number of pages devoted to a particular set will show instantly which sets require the most attention and, correspondingly, money.

For example, in the entire script, INT RESTAURANT may have 3–2/8 pages during the day, then another 16–4/8 pages at night; your total page count for that set would be 19–6/8. *Page count is important because it will crystallize your priorities by showing you the weight of work that takes place in each set.* Experience will tell you when you may combine scenes, possibly saving time and money.

After you have prepared your own breakdown sheet, you will meet with your Construction Coordinator to gauge labour and materials costs. There are many schools of thought here; basically, you will need a budgeting formula, such as 70 per cent labour and 30 per cent materials.

'Fringe' benefits/costs can affect a budget tremendously (studio or location charges and/or rebates offered by states and countries); speak to the Accounting Department to add them in later.

Always tell Production upfront that you don't estimate costs for fringes, as they vary a great deal.

Then, you will further refine your formula to account for contingencies, changes, and so on.

Especially in the early stages of preparing your budget breakdown, it's best to *plan responsibly.* Unforeseen challenges will inevitably arise.

Because they are in charge of the sets and locations, Production Designers have the unique opportunity to offer time- and/or money-saving alternatives that may creatively improve a project.

For example, on the movie *The Beguiled*, Production Designer Ted Haworth became a hero when he offered a time-saving economy for the opening sequence, which originally called for the filming of a civil war battle. He created a collage of Mathew Brady photographs for the camera to pan, one of which had a striking resemblance to one of the film's stars, Clint Eastwood. The result was successful and saved much-needed dollars for the rest of the picture.

Calendar/Shooting Schedule (time management; work backwards from shoot dates)

Master Calendar

You will need to **set up a calendar** specifically for all Art Department functions. This is a calendar that is separate from the shooting schedule but must be compatible with it. This calendar should clearly show—at a glance—the **prep dates**, **shoot dates**, and **strike dates**, among other information, such as **D/N (day/night)**, **INT/EXT (interior/exterior)**, and **STG/LOC (stage/location)**.

Within this calendar will be your own **subset of deadlines and notes** for construction. These include notes for:

- Paint and wallpaper
- Finishes
- Location prep
- Sign shop orders (pick up, installation, and strike)
- Any miniatures or backings
- Greens
- Miscellaneous details.

The usual method is to hang large calendar pages (or dry-erase calendars) on the wall where all can see. Each week and month of shooting should be represented. Coloured post-its marking INT/EXT sets, D/NSTG/LOC and any other speciality notes (such as 'backings delivered', etc.) should be placed on the calendars. **This calendar will become invaluable** and will be used by all who enter the Art Department. Each department can easily refer to the master calendar as questions arise about set dressing, rigging, lighting, striking, and so on. The calendar also shows which departments are working on the sets and when.

Using this calendar, you will need to **collaborate** and **discuss scheduling** with your set decorator often and regularly, because your two departments will work together extremely closely. The Set Decorating Department needs to have the sets camera-ready **before** shooting. They need time to install window treatments, hang light fixtures, and hang artwork, in addition to placing all furnishings.

Figure 2.7 A master show calendar

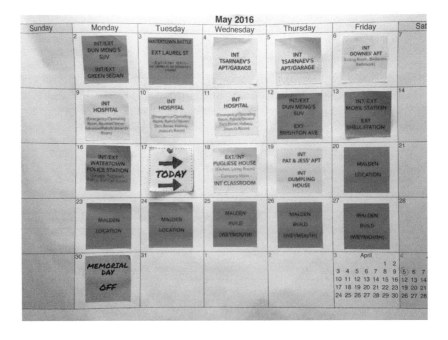

This calendar is an essential tool for an **organized, smooth-running** Art Department. Develop a system that shows your workflow on the calendar, and be sure that everyone in the Art Department understands it. The master calendar will be in use when you are not around, so *it is crucial that your system is clear, easy to read, and easy to comprehend*.

The post-its can be moved around as changes inevitably occur, and the colours help identify the types of sets and scenes at a glance (for example, blue post-its could mean NIGHT shooting).

Shooting Schedule

The **shooting schedule** is the map for the entire production; it addresses every detail and requirement for each department.

The **one liner schedule** is based on the full shooting schedule, and is the schedule most often used and revised.

This includes the availability of actors, equipment rentals, locations, crew parking, transportation and drivers, vehicles, crew meals, and the scenes to be filmed. EVERY DAY. FOR THE ENTIRE SHOOT!

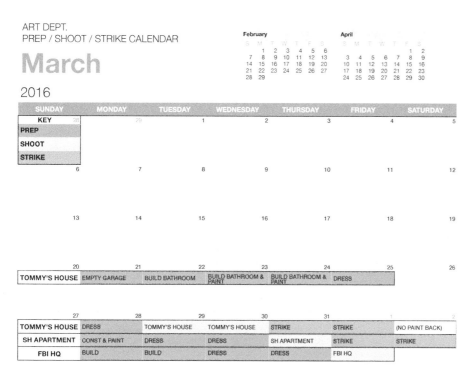

Figure 2.8 A show calendar: Prep–Shoot–Strike

Figure 2.8 Continued

ART DEPT.
PREP / SHOOT / STRIKE CALENDAR

April
2016

March						
S	M	T	W	T	F	S
		1	2	3	4	5
6	7	8	9	10	11	12
13	14	15	16	17	18	19
20	21	22	23	24	25	26
27	28	29	30	31		

May						
S	M	T	W	T	F	S
1	2	3	4	5	6	7
8	9	10	11	12	13	14
15	16	17	18	19	20	21
22	23	24	25	26	27	28
29	30	31				

SUNDAY	MONDAY	TUESDAY	WEDNESDAY	THURSDAY	FRIDAY	SATURDAY
KEY 27	28 · Prep Tommy's House · FBI	29 · FBI	30 · FBI · Dingy Stairwell	31 · FBI	1 · Conn Rob @ Gym / Bathroom	2
PREP					· FBI · Black Falcon	
SHOOT		· Tommy's House	· Tommy's House	· Dingy Stairwell		
STRIKE				· Tommy's House	· Dingy Stairwell · Tommy's House	
3	4 · Black Falcon Change Overs · Bathroom (Gram)	5 · Black Falcon Change Overs	6 · Black Falcon Change Overs	7 · Black Falcon Change Overs	8 · Arsenal Mall - Tents	9
	· Black Falcon · FBI	· Black Falcon · Bathroom · FBI	· Black Falcon	· Black Falcon	· Black Falcon	
10	11 · Arsenal Mall · Boat Owner's	12 · Boat Owner's	13 · Boat Owner's · Doyle's	14 · Boat Owner's · Doyle's	15 · Boat Owner's	16
	· Black Falcon	· Arsenal Mall	· Arsenal Mall	· Ext Black Falcon · Doyle's	· Collier's Apt	
				· Arsenal Mall	· Arsenal Mall	
17	18 · Boat Owner's · Tsarnaev Apt	19 · Tsarnaev Apt	20 · Tsarnaev Apt · Dorm Dress · Marathon Vendors	21 · Dorm Dress · Marathon Vendors	22 · Dorm Dress · Marathon Vendors	23 · Marathon Vendors
	MARATHON	· Boat Owner's	· Boat Owner's	· Boat Owner's	· Ext MIT	
					· Boat Owner's	
24 · Weymouth Night · Changeover · Malden Loc	25 26 · Weymouth Night · Changeover · Malden Loc		27 · Malden Loc	28 · Malden Loc	29 · Malden Loc	30
· Weymouth: PRE-Bombing	· Weymouth: POST-Bombing	· Weymouth: POST-Bombing	· Weymouth: POST-Bombing	· Weymouth: POST-Bombing		
· Boat Owner's	· Boat Owner's					

ART DEPT.
PREP / SHOOT / STRIKE CALENDAR

May
2016

April						
S	M	T	W	T	F	S
					1	2
3	4	5	6	7	8	9
10	11	12	13	14	15	16
17	18	19	20	21	22	23
24	25	26	27	28	29	30

June						
S	M	T	W	T	F	S
			1	2	3	4
5	6	7	8	9	10	11
12	13	14	15	16	17	18
19	20	21	22	23	24	25
26	27	28	29	30		

SUNDAY	MONDAY	TUESDAY	WEDNESDAY	THURSDAY	FRIDAY	SATURDAY
KEY 1	2 · Hospital	3 · Hospital	4 · Hospital	5 · Hospital	6 · Hospital · Mobil (Day Off)	7
PREP						
SHOOT	· Malden Loc · Auto Shop	· Malden Loc	· Malden Loc	· Malden Loc	· Mobil / Shell Station	
STRIKE					· Mobil (Day Off) · Malden Loc	
8	9	10	11 · Watertown Police Station	12 · Watertown Police Station	13 · Watertown Police Station	14
	· Hospital	· Hospital	· Hospital	· Dun Meng's SUV · Green Sedan	· Dun Meng's SUV · Brighton Ave	
	· Malden "Laurel St"	· Malden "Laurel St"		· Hospital	· Hospital	
15	16 · Watertown Police Station	17	18 · Pugliese's House	19	20	21
	· Dun Meng's SUV · Brighton Ave	· Watertown Police Station	· Dunkin Donuts · Pugliese's Van	· Pugliese's House · Classroom	· WEYMOUTH: Malden Shootout	
			· Watertown Police Station	· Watertown Police Station		
22	23	24	25 · MIT Campus - Lab · UMASS - Dorm	26 · Downe's Home · Subway, Railcar	27 · Dumpling House	28
	· Tsarnaev Apt	· Tsarnaev Apt	· Tsarnaev Apt	· Tsarnaev Apt		
29	30 MEMORIAL DAY OFF	31	1	2	3	4

It is an extraordinary, difficult, complex task, which falls traditionally to the First AD (Assistant Director), who is familiar with literally every nuance of every faction of the show.

Changes are constantly a part of this; and, like a rubric cube, one small change will affect the entire schedule.

It can be frustrating as well as challenging, and takes a certain personality to actually enjoy dealing with this monster!

In the old days, these shooting schedules were done on large boards with coloured strips, interchangeable and moveable whenever an actor got sick or a location dropped out of play.

Today, these schedules are still meticulous nightmares to produce, but they can be done digitally, which enables making changes and publishing much easier.

It is _essential_ that you have and maintain a close relationship with the First AD at all times.

Not only to _get_ the most current information about the shoot, but also to _give_ them progress reports and making them aware of any delays/alterations you might anticipate, no matter how seemingly insignificant to you.

This is a good habit to develop, also, because you may learn something _in advance,_ such as, they're adding another day to the current location, which gives you and the Set Dec team another day to prep the next set.

The schedule has a domino effect, one change alters many … sometimes for days or even weeks, and sometimes a simple change may result in cuts or new sets/locations; even re-writing of the script. For example, if the cafe location is no longer available on the shooting day, can it be re-written as a 'walk and talk' in a park, or on a nearby beach?

Your AD will also work to help you, shooting 'around' that missing miniature, or offering to schedule an insert shot later on, when something goes awry and your key item doesn't make it to the set on time.

Every fragment of every scene is reflected in the shooting schedule.

Props are listed, stunts are noted, cast members and call times are published.

The First AD deserves respect for quick-thinking and for having as much knowledge (sometimes more) about the production than the Director.

Once the shooting schedule is 'locked' (based on a 'locked' script), it is approved by Production, published and distributed to the entire production crew.

This guides the production and acts as an outline for the progress expected of the company, day by day.

From this master shooting schedule, the daily **'call sheets'** are prepared, listing, in addition to the day's locations or stages, the _scene numbers_ expected to be completed that day, whether the shots are to be filmed _Day or Night_, _Interior/Exterior_, and every specific detail needed for that day's shoot (fog machine, for example, or school bus).

- Special vehicles are noted (with their own 'call times')
- Special wardrobe notes (multiple takes, blood, etc.)
- SP FX (bullet hits, smoke, fog, green or blue screen)
- Company moves are noted (with approximate times)
- Crew parking location
- If shooting on location, 'load in' and 'load out' times are noted (different for every county)
- Nearest hospital (even though a medic is always on set)

- Sunrise and sunset times are noted (mostly for the Cinematography team, but nice to know).

And if this isn't enough, some ADs even find time to add a quote of the day or trivia question, just to keep things interesting!

Not only does the call sheet have to be completely accurate, leaving nothing out for the next day, but it must be prepared and ready to distribute by the end of the day's shoot!!!

The call sheet tells everyone what the call time will be for the next day, where they must report for work, and what to prepare for in advance.

You can appreciate the level of communication and organization needed to accomplish this feat, day after day, during or while shooting a full 12-hour day on set.

It is worth noting, the First AD deserves your respect and collaboration; develop the habit of regularly touching base, even if you have nothing to say but a kind word or clever bit of humour.

The acknowledgement will be appreciated, and will work in your favour when you may need one.

You, as PD, want to build a reputation of being the solid, confident rock they can depend on. This will guarantee work in your future.

By the way, at the top of this all-important daily call sheet is the show or production's logo, which has been designed by you and approved by the Director—usually within your first week on the project.

The **show logo** is one design that cannot wait; try to begin formulating one immediately in your mind, after first reading the script. It has to be simple, graphic, appropriate, and easy to read and print.

This logo gives the show an immediate *identity*; it validates the project and will be printed on business cards, vehicle cards (for dashboards, identifying cast and crew), office and room labels, crew T-shirts, jackets, stationery, cast and crew lists, etc.

Have one or two examples or rough ideas to show the Director, and allow them to choose. *This establishes the way you two will work as a team throughout the production—* don't overlook the importance of this seemingly minor detail!!!

Including your Director in the identity of the show is a critical part of your relationship; always get approval for every design decision.

To quote Tom Duffield (*Lone Survivor*, *Patriots Day*, *Hell or High Water*, *Ed Wood*), **NO SURPRISES**! This will not only protect you, but will ensure a collaborative process between you and your Director.

> You have to please the people with the money, because without the money, nothing moves.
>
> You know, you learn your lesson with money, with big money, and the manipulation of it in relation to design. But each time the problem comes up, it comes in a new costume, with new masks, and you have to be ready.
>
> Give them an honest budget. You have to level; it takes a lot of talking. You have to be right in there with the Director and the Producer.
>
> —John DeCuir, Sr (*Cleopatra, Hello Dolly, The King and I*)

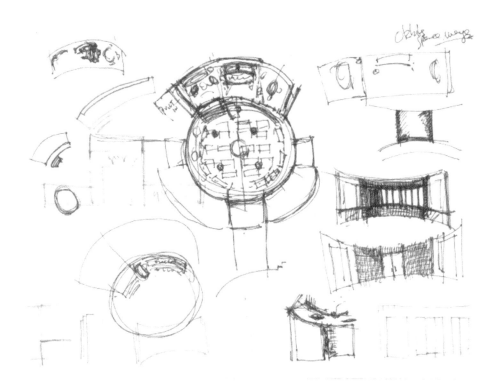

Figure 2.9 *Hidden Figures*, sketch

Figure 2.10 *Hidden Figures*, space task group Lorez

CHAPTER 3

Pre-Production—Locations and Research

We needed a location on this picture I was working on, and the location team and I looked for weeks but couldn't find anything—I knew exactly what I wanted; it had to look like 1940s' Los Angeles. It was frustrating, because we were running out of time.

One evening, my date and I were driving home through Hollywood on an unexpected street, and suddenly I saw it! STOP THE CAR!!!

I got out and knew that I had found our location; it was perfect.

I wasn't looking—but *I knew what it was when I found it.*

I had dreamed about it every night for weeks, so that when I saw it, I was ready.

—Jeannine Oppewal (*LA Confidential, Pleasantville,*
Catch Me If You Can, Seabiscuit)

Figure 3.0 Location,
Magnificent Obsession

In this chapter we will cover all aspects of filming on location, including selecting a location, gathering information on it, and treating the location with respect. You'll become familiar with the basic differences between interior sets and exterior locations and the considerations relating to sensitive and remote locations. It's up to you—the Production Designer—to make a location work and provide everything the Director and the script call for.

Figure 3.1 Downton Abbey, EXT, Lady Violet's residence

Menzies was an amazing man. He used to do things like, if there was not enough money to build a whole exterior of a church and a monk is coming out of the front door of the church, he would do things like, literally lock the camera off, build *just the stairway needed,* whether its 3 or 4 steps.

He would build the base of a door; the door would be thick with a piece of hardware on it.

It was massive, but he would never build that door *two inches above* what the camera would see.

In order to give it the feeling of a church, give it the scale, <u>*he forced your imagination to do that*</u>.

He would take pigeons and put them on the top step, eating away, and there's that door swung open, very slowly, because it's a hundred, imagine, a hundred feet high.

A tired old hand of a Jesuit opens it and the pigeons would fly off and the man would walk into the foreground or down the steps or whatever he was supposed to do with the scene, but it was locked off because the economics were locked off.

You could not build the door 100 feet high, so he made you <u>think</u> it was 100 feet high with the depth of the door and the hardware and the steps in the foreground.

It was a marvellous device.

—*Ted Haworth (Strangers on a Train, Some Like It Hot,*
Longest Day, Marty)

Having the action in the script broken down prior to scouting is a must in selecting locations.

The input of the Director of Photography (DP) deserves mention here; very often it is the DP who decides if a location is acceptable. The direction of the sunlight, how many hours of daylight or night time and the ability to bring in lighting equipment are all part of the decision process. If the Designer is aware of the lighting issues, it can save a lot of time scouting locations.

Figure 3.2 Abu Dhabi storefront used as Ext. Internet Cafe

Figure 3.3 (a) Abandoned Phoenix Ice Factory transformed into Int. Internet Cafe

Figure 3.3 (b) The internet cafe set being dressed (on location), *The Kingdom*

Location Scout

> Every choice you make is you. They are interested in what the scene means.
> —Dick Sylbert (*The Graduate, Baby Doll, Chinatown, Rosemary's Baby, Dick Tracy*)

Shooting on location brings its own special set of requirements and challenges. A location is a set, but it is not on a stage. Often, it is in someone's home, workplace, or neighbourhood.

The initial location scouting is usually one of the first tasks a Production Designer is required to participate in, either on their own or with a **Location Manager** hired by the production company. Eventually, there will be a van and driver, Production Manager or Producer, and the Director, along with the First AD (Assistant Director)—they are all part of this 'Location Scout' group. As a group, you will visit several locations in a day, all prescheduled and prearranged by the **Location Manager**.

This initial van ride together presents a wonderful opportunity for you to discuss the script with the Director. Before you arrive at the location, you will discover the Director's ideas for filming and blocking each scene.

Experience will tell you quickly whether or not a particular location is a good fit for the requirements. If the location is approved by the team, your first task is to photograph and measure the area to be used for filming. If possible, ask the Director to identify the left edge and right edge of the framing. This will limit your scope of responsibilities for prepping the area. Often, the left right edges of the framing may change for a variety of reasons. It is always a good idea to be prepared for an expansion of what the camera will see.

Blazing Saddles: Locations

by Production Designer Peter Wooley

We shot all the day exteriors locally.

The opening shot was at both Vasquez Rocks (a well-known location, shot a zillion times) and in Rosamond, out in the Mojave Desert beyond Palmdale and Lancaster.

The last shot in the picture—the limo drives off—was shot in Rosamond.

The 'You do that voodoo that you do so well!!' sequence was also at Vasquez Rocks, as well as the registration sequence: 'Where are all the white women at?'

The town of Rockridge was the Western street at Warner Bros. I added a few buildings at the end of the 'street', then I took those buildings out to the desert, so when the bad guys ride into town to 'Rape all the cattle and stampede the women', and the buildings fall down there is only desert and cattle behind them. Couldn't pull that off on the back lot.

All the night exterior sequences were shot on the stage; the famous farting scene was an interior. 'More beans, Mr. Taggert?'

All interiors were built on the stage.

I tried to design this as a real movie Western, but screwed around just slightly with a cartoon look. I only painted a few buildings in Rockridge cartoon colors. The saloon was bright red, and the interior (on a stage) was slightly 'over the top'. Real, but silly real.

I had to put an orange top on Howard Johnson's Ice Cream Parlor, and paint 'One Flavor' on the window. Never pass up a joke.

The scenes just before the end of the film were actually shot—exterior and interior—at Grauman's Chinese Theater. I matched the carpet in the lobby so we could put cattle in there and not have to clean their carpets of 'cow poop'. Tell me show business isn't glamorous.

Really, for me, the hardest thing about designing this film was walking that 'cartoon line'.

I didn't want the images we make fighting with the lyrics of the script.

Blazing Saddles is so far over the top that I felt it should be grounded in … 'sorta' reality.

Sounds obscure, but …

Funny, Mel and I never really talked about that. He liked everything I gave him, and, as far as I can remember, never turned down a single thing. I don't think that happens too often.

Funny, hell, he even liked my sketches of the dance number, 'Doing the French Mistake' with Dommie. I built it, we shot it, next. Funny.

Looking at Mel's first two pictures before BS for research on how he worked, I noticed his tendency to stage and shoot in 'proscenium'. That is, he tended to stage things like a stage play; enter/exit stage right or left, line up the actors and let 'em talk.

I tried to design to make him comfortable, and he staged like that.

Funny, again, we never talked that much about it. Subsequent films got him outta the habit.

Thank God.

> Peter Wooley, Production Designer (*Blazing Saddles*,
> *High Anxiety*, *The Day After*)

Recording as much information as possible on this first visit will prove very valuable later on in the production process.

Once the main locations have been narrowed down and selected, the **Location Manager** makes the deals with the appropriate representatives. Contracts are signed and the *shooting schedule* can be built around these agreements.

Again, <u>always allow for the possibility of change</u>. Be flexible. **Nothing is certain until the final signatures are on the page. Always keep your 'plan B' options open until you have confirmation from the Producer that your locations are locked.**

Scout Notes from *Hell or High Water* (Production Designer Tom Duffield)

Art Scout Notes

OLNEY BANK @ PORTALES (OPTICIANS).

More walls to paint per the sample colour, including our **door cover flat**.

2 door openings to plug, using borrowed doors that are not seen.

Match for honey woodwork is EARLY AMERICAN/PROVINCIAL.

JAYTON BANK @ PORTALES

Bank sign now hanging in front of window under roof.

Our Texas road sign mount on existing pole.

ARCHER BANK @ SUDDEN LINK

Our two large exterior signs will need be struck, and refitted again for later shoot date.

More walls to paint per two selected sample colours. Green wall goes to darker colour. Space is 18' {x} 24' approx.

Match existing colours for possible renovation.

Poss. 4' 6" {x} 5' 6" {x} 2' 2" painted ply cover to make. Discuss.

12" {x} 18" sign.

B. Clausen Reserved parking. Sign 8" {x} 20" (nom). Required.

POST BANK (Shoot out)

3/4" balsa panels to make for bullet hits. {x} 4

1/2" balsa letter racks for hits also.

1/2" painted foam core required to cover existing signage.

Parking lot gravel for side walk ramp up.

VERNON BANK (1208 Main)

Renovate curbs to match drive through area.

Blue ext. panel is going to need paint/hole filling.

MDF parking sign.

New interior colour #1545 IRON GATE. Room is 24' {x} 35' {x} 14' high. **Virtually entire space needs paint.**

Including small office to left.

VERNON DINER

Owner is replacing a window for us.

Poss. an exterior door to paint. (Tagged)

POST BANK (Shoot out)

3/4" balsa panels to make for bullet hits. {x} 4

1/2" balsa letter racks for hits also.

1/2" painted foam core required to cover existing signage across street.

Parking lot gravel for side walk ram

Also:

Additional city road sign added. (Highway Supply Company?)

Figure 3.4 Location,
research spotting plan,
Hell or High Water

Location vs Stage

I believe if you're going to do your finest dramatic job, you're going to have to acquire a stage and work under <u>controlled conditions</u>.

Nature has great beauty, but it isn't always controllable.

John DeCuir, Sr (*Cleopatra, Hello Dolly, The King and I*)

Think of your favourite TV shows. On these shows, what is the ratio of stage sets to location sets? In other words, how much of the show is filmed on interior sets, compared to exterior locations?

Some shows are filmed entirely on locations, which become sets (e.g. *Survivor*), while some shows are filmed almost entirely on stage sets (e.g. *How I Met Your Mother*). These stage sets have a few **second unit** location shots (exteriors), usually of a city, building, or possibly a travelling vehicle (bus or train).

A second unit is a film crew separate from the main crew that gets miscellaneous shots without the leading cast.

These second unit location shots don't contain the principal actors. They are strictly there to provide relief from an all-interior show. Without these brief exterior shots, we would feel confined. It's natural to want to cut outside for a breath of fresh air. Be sure you allow for some balance on your projects.

Location Logistics 1

Once you have arrived at a possible new location and everyone gets out of the van to have a look, you have to **quickly record** all of the details of the location while **listening closely** to what the Director and Cinematographer say about the location. Multitasking and juggling are valuable skills in Production Design. **It's up to YOU to make this a working location and to provide everything the script calls for** (and everything the Director has asked you to provide).

This is <u>your</u> responsibility, no one else's. Everyone else might be looking around, thinking about the scenes or their lunch. **You**, as the Production Designer, are thinking, planning, and designing all that is needed to make the location serve the script. The script has definite points of action that the location must fulfil. You will need to consider accommodating the crews, the shooting company, and the actors. You will also need to consider the **logistics of making the site easily accessible**. Your great responsibility is to create the **physical environment**.

You may have only a week to get the location ready, **minus** the time your set decorator, grip and electric, greens person, etc. need to prep and load in. This is **lightning speed**, but you will **develop a rhythm**. Like a chef in a top restaurant, you must be quick and fast, accurate, and on point, and you

Figure 3.5 Location, *Babe (Ruth) Comes Home* (1927)

must enjoy the pace, because it never lets up. Once a television series begins shooting, it is **like a high-speed train coming down the tracks**, and your job is to stay ahead of it and prepare the way. Time is money, and it stops for no one. **Educate yourself to be efficient**, and you won't have to drive back to that location to measure the windows in your own time. Instead, you'll remember to get it all down the first time.

Location Logistics 2

The best way to be sure you've covered everything you may need on a location scout is to **bring your script with you** and be sure to read every detail. Ask the Director how they plan to shoot the scenes, and accommodate every requirement.

Note: In film, location scouts can go on for months, because film crews have the **time** and **money** to find exactly the right place. This allows for more research, as well as the additional time needed to find something that works perfectly for everyone.

In television, location scouting is accelerated. You may only get **one chance** to visit the location, so you need to be on your game. This means you are measuring, photographing, matching paint colours, and making notes, all while paying attention to what the Director is saying. Sometimes, even after a location has been decided on and you have planned and prepared for it, for some reason, that particular location cannot be used. It's back to square one, and the clock is ticking, because **in television, shooting never stops**.

Figure 3.6 *Seabiscuit*, location notes, J. Oppewall

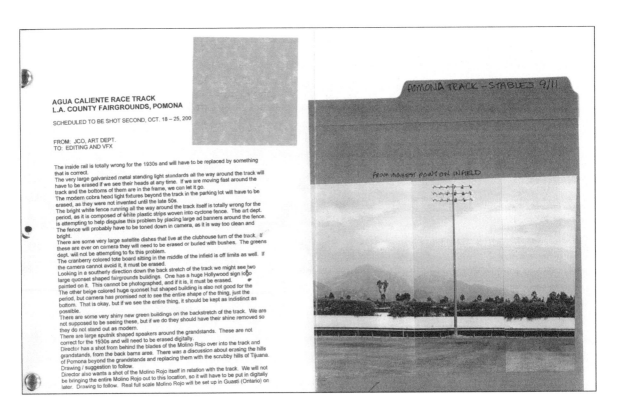

You may have to leave the current episode you're prepping to view another location and make another choice, or you may be asked to choose from the Location Manager's photos without actually visiting the location (never a good idea). Regardless, you should **always** be an active participant in the location choices!

Sometimes, everyone, including the Director, will **love** a location and think that it's perfect, but you, and only you, will **have to make that location work**, because you have to think about the bigger picture. What needs to be built? What will be delivered? How elaborate is the setup? What needs to be painted, modified, dressed, or undressed? You are responsible for **every detail** related to the scenes shot at the location.

Remember: **Never compromise to please someone if it's against your better judgement. Hold out for what you know to be right; you will be respected for it.**

The Scout Bag

To make the most of your time on a location scout, always carry a **'scout bag'**. This should hold a fan deck of **paint colours**, **graph paper**, pens and pencils, a **camera (and a back-up and batteries, in case a camera fails)**, **a 25-foot tape measure** (100 feet for fields and larger areas) or a **laser measuring device** (faster and can measure areas that a tape won't reach) and, if you really want to be thorough, a **compass**. This is in addition to the usual **mobile phone**, **notepad**, **script**, **water bottle**, and **hat**.

This is the process you should follow for every location scout:

1. Take **photographs** from each of the four corners (see the following video).
2. Quickly sketch a freehand layout of the **floor plan**.
3. **Identify architectural features**: columns, fireplace, windows, doors, stairs, etc. **Label the plan** with scene numbers, day/night, and interior/exterior.
4. **Add any callouts** (a list of **modifications**/work notes for each department) to your plan, including:
   - Paint
   - Construction
   - Camera
   - Action/stunts
   - **Signs, wild (or breakaway) walls**, etc.

Additionally, try to give some **sense of scale** (overall dimensions of width x length) and compass **direction** (N, S, E, or W). Remember to **spot** everything—i.e. identify the location of important things such as columns, trees, fountains, etc.—according to the script and the Director's blocking.

Blocking refers to the positioning and movement of actors in a scene. Since the camera can move as well, blocking in cinema also includes blocking for the camera.

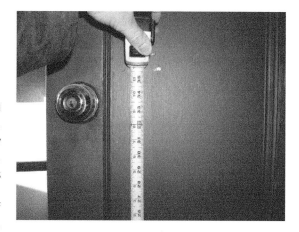

Figure 3.7 Location, measuring height of doorknob

Figure 3.8 Location plan, *Hell or High Water*, with Call Outs

Trench Layout

Location Basics

A location is like another character in the script—always try to make it the very best! **Some basics:**

- When scouting locations, **be open to new ideas**. You may have something very clearly outlined in your mind; however, if you find a location that fits all requirements but it is different from your initial concept, go with it! Often, you'll find something unique that may be easier on the budget, or perhaps is located closer to the production's home base.
- **Don't be overly swayed** by a Location Manager's opinions (e.g. 'It's easier, cheaper, looks OK', etc.). The Location Manager's primary concern is locking down the location. It's **your** responsibility to hold out for **exactly** what you have in mind and think will work best.
- **Never compromise on space** (you always need more than you think) or on the main elements you need for each particular set.
- **Locations are usually unalterable** (or alterable for a price), so you must weigh the amount of work a space needs against the time and costs of building the set onstage.

Figure 3.9 Location, *Hell or High Water*, trench with half car buried in it

Location Set Etiquette

Set Etiquette

Think of a location as a temporary set. Everything must come in and out, with the conditions **exactly as you found them** (or even better). Follow these practices:

- **Be respectful!** Treat each location as though it were your home, and expect the crew to do the same.
- **DO NOT sit or stand** on beds, furniture, open closets, etc.

You are representing the production company and the film studio. Your reputation is on the line, so be sure your crew (and all crews) are briefed on proper set etiquette before and during filming (i.e. no sleeping on sofas, no food or drinks on set, no smoking on set, etc.).

ALWAYS PROTECT YOURSELF! Remember:

- If **painting** is allowed at a location, be sure to **get it in writing**, i.e. get it in the contract with the owner (so you aren't surprised at the end with a bill to 'restore to original colour').
- Make sure **everything** that needs to be done to your location is **APPROVED and CLEARED** with the Producers, Location Manager, and client (location owner).

BE PROFESSIONAL!

The first thing your crew should do is **prep the location** by covering the floors with something protective like **layout board** (heavy cardboard). Furniture pads are not acceptable because you can trip on them—they are a liability, and using them is a sure sign of an amateur.

PROTECT YOUR SET!

Be vigilant about placement of everything that is part of the set and be clear about who is allowed to touch or handle what.

Hot set signs should be posted during filming to alert everyone that the set is **active and in use**. Nothing should be touched or moved, because that would affect continuity in the scene.

Wrap/Location

Try to **leave the location in better condition** than you found it. Be generous. This ensures a good reputation (in case you ever need to come back) and paves the way for future filming. Other companies will hear about you, so be sure all you leave behind is good will.

Miscellaneous

Filming in neighbourhoods comes with some challenges. Note that you may encounter any of the following:

- Lawnmower or leaf blower (just as camera is rolling, someone starts up a LOUD machine)
- Loud radio played by the neighbours (or musicians)
- People hoping to get into the movies
- Spoilers (gossips) who spread untrue rumours and disrupt the company.

Be aware of the hours when filming is permitted—each location is different. Every city has its own hours and requirements; be aware of these and respect them! Any abuse of these rules, however minor it may seem, could lead to fines and/or cancellation of the privilege of filming there. You are representing a film company; remember that your actions will affect future filmmaking opportunities.

There are hours for **loading in** and **loading out**, which are different from actual filming hours, so make sure you know **when** your crew can arrive with a truck and **how late in the evening** the crew can load up. This will affect your scheduling and timing for getting sets ready or wrapping up. If the neighbourhood doesn't allow trucks to move after 7 pm, you will cost the company another day's rental if you do not plan ahead.

Additional Location Notes

Location Notes

Locations can be fun and challenging once you are familiar with the logistics. They often provide **opportunities to be creative in unusual places**. For example, *Melrose Place* had a different cafe or restaurant scene written into nearly every episode. Shooting in actual locations was expensive because the production had to buy out the entire restaurant for at least two days—one day to prep and one day to shoot.

The Producers were looking for an affordable solution, and came to the **Art Department** for suggestions. After looking at the shooting schedule, it became clear that 'creating' new restaurants on the stage location would be the most economical. There was no room on any of their stages to build more sets, but outside was a big, open parking lot.

After discussing the costs with **Set Dressing** to bring in tables, chairs, linens, glassware, etc., with **props** for food, flowers, menus, and silverware, and with the **Greens Department** to bring in hedges, vines, arbours, and flowers, it was determined that the Art Department could 'create' an outdoor cafe for a fraction of the cost of filming on location. In addition, this would save a **company move**, a costly activity, which eats up time because each department has to pack up and load their trucks, drive to another location, park again, unload, etc.

The **Art Department** on *Melrose Place* became known for building 'parking lot cafes' in record time. They were challenged from then on to top themselves and to create something new and different every week. It became a game to guess what they would come up with next!

As the Production Designer, it is up to you to be creative when offering solutions to any challenge.

Some locations are sensitive and require special considerations. Other locations are remote, meaning they are too far away to commute to on a daily basis.

'Sensitive' Locations:

- Quiet neighbourhoods, schools, offices
- Churches, convents, temples, cemeteries, retirement homes
- Family homes (family lives there during prep, shoot, and wrap)
- Beaches, airports, hotels.

Remote Locations:

- Far from home
- Passports required
- Currency exchange is necessary.

Be sure that **accommodation for travel is covered**. Per diem stipends cover your meals. You should know whether you will:

- Have a 6- or 7-day work week (are Saturdays and Sundays required?)
- Need transportation (will you get a car?)
- Hire crew locally or bring them with you (e.g. Art Director, Set Designer, Construction Coordinator, painter, etc.)
- Have a special pay rate (for working away from home).

CHAPTER 4

Art Department and Storyboards

Art Department

We play a key part in the unified direction that any film takes.

In order to get a unified direction for the film, it will often rest on our shoulders to get that unity, to give the picture a direction, and we hope that it will be the right one.

—Bob Boyle (*North by Northwest, Cape Fear, Thomas Crown Affair, The Birds*)

This chapter will emphasize the three Cs of any project: collaborating, communicating, and clarity. The duties of every member of the Art Department and how they interact with each other will be explained. Related departments will be included, as they are often integral to the design process.

The Art of Production Design

The approach to designing or finding the look is always the same, no matter the project: you search, research, and **open your mind and senses** to anything and everything you can find that may be pertinent to your project. And then—often when you are not looking for it—you find that one perfect image that is absolutely right on every level.

When this happens, you just *know* it's right.

Often, the off times are when inspiration occurs. Learn to trust this inspiration! Don't overthink this part of the job, because it is more than just facts; it involves emotions. This phase should be fun and creative; it's why Production Design is called an **art**.

Every project is different. Every challenge is different. But the process remains the same. You immerse yourself in the written world (the story or **script**), your Director communicates their **emotional point of view** (their **vision**), and *your job is to marry the two appropriately.* Then you allow the magic to happen—the magic of designing **the look**, the magic that is **the power of visuals**.

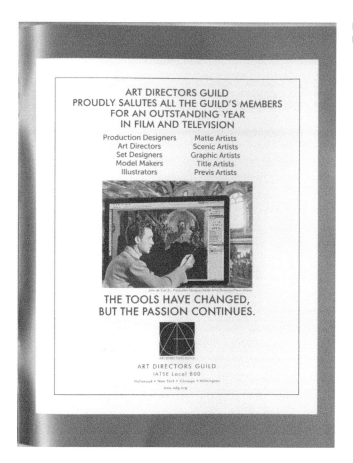

Figure 4.1 Art Department/ADG

Figure 4.2 *Star Wars* Art Department, left to right: Stephen Childs, Alan Roderick Jones, Harry Lange, Stephen Cooper, Ted Ambrose

Professionalism

There are no shortcuts to being *respectful* and *responsible!*

Professionalism (1)

In the old studio system under a supervising Art Director, you worked all the time. The studio system was like a factory, turning out movies quickly and regularly.

Today, the motion picture business is a people business; **you are always a freelancer**, going from one project to the next, sometimes across town, or to another state, or even to another country. Presenting yourself in a professional way—with confidence and a clear, authentic brand or style—**should begin now**.

Your colleagues become your best referrals and sources for your next job. Communication, integrity, and 'playing well in the sandbox' are nearly as important as talent—employers are looking for a combination of these qualities.

If you do well, get along with others, show up on time, never go over budget, accept changes cheerfully, and show resourcefulness and flexibility at all times, you will be remembered and appreciated. A good attitude, enthusiasm, and energy are welcomed, especially when long hours and short tempers prevail.

In the old studio system, Art Directors wore suits and ties; today, Designers have the freedom to brand themselves with personal style, as did Richard Sylbert, with his safari jacket uniform, or Jeannine Oppewall, with her signature red lipstick.

Because it is a *collaborative business*, everyone that you meet and work with has the power to recommend you, sometimes even from another department. Each of those people knows at least 10 others; this is called **networking**, so be sure to bring your 'A-game' from day one! Make it a habit so that you don't have to think about it. It will become natural to **be on time**, to **over-deliver**, to **meet deadlines**, to **follow through**, to **resist gossip**, to **be prepared**, to **anticipate needs**, to **project a positive attitude**, and so on.

Ask yourself: **Would *you* hire you?**

Professionalism (2)

From a production standpoint, aside from your talent, bringing your work in **on time** and **on budget** will always equal steady work. *Respecting deadlines and budget constraints is paramount to every professional in the film industry.*

Changes are part of the game; they happen regularly and for many reasons. Accept them gracefully and without complaint, be flexible and resourceful, and you will quickly become a valued member of the team.

Often, it is the most talented and celebrated person in the room who is open, willing, and secure enough to accept suggestions or new ideas from anyone and everyone. Again, this is the mark of a true professional. Learn from their example.

'There are no problems, only solutions' is an oft-repeated mantra. Instead of thinking of something as a problem, accept it as a challenge and find a solution. Adopting this attitude is the mark of a true professional.

Even on your first day working on a project, you are 'interviewing' for future jobs based on your energy, attitude, and work ethic, regardless of experience.

People remember what you do and how you react under pressure.

Follow these practices:

- Volunteer
- Ask questions
- Come in early
- Show an interest
- Always put in effort.

A logo/brand design or original business card is an easy way to make an impression; this *is* a **design** field. Make sure your contact information is current, memorable, and accurate. Typos imply carelessness, and carelessness implies laziness. Proofread everything!

Most of all, remember to have fun!

Art Department

The Art Department is the Production Designer's responsibility. Usually, the Production Designer will be allowed to hire the team members. This team will include:

- Art Director
- Set Designer
- Set Decorator
- Prop Master
- Construction Coordinator
- Sometimes, an Art Department Coordinator
- Sometimes, a Graphic Designer.

Each position is vital, and many departments overlap in their duties. All of them report to you.

Figure 4.3 Home office, T. Duffield, Research

Figure 4.4 Town model,
designers discussion

Art Department Duties—Research

Refining your research is an important part of achieving 'the look'. You might start with a hundred pieces of research and reduce them to the ten that are the most appropriate to the look. 'Less is more' often applies and is a good rule to follow. Paying attention to the many small details (such as a small hand prop, for example) can suddenly become **extremely** important in a close-up. Make it count!

Every day (at least once a day) in the Art Department, your assistant (Art Director or Set Designer) will have a briefing with you, the Production Designer, and this assistant will **carry out management duties for the various projects** in the works.

Some of these duties include:

- Monitoring Set Designers and fielding any of their questions
- Hiring and monitoring Storyboard Artists and/or Graphic Artists
- Balancing the budget for sets and changes
- Checking progress on sign orders and designs
- Gathering research from the best sources available
- Taking photographs and measuring any locations
- Selecting, ordering, and scheduling backings

- Staying current with the office paperwork, updated script pages, etc.
- Communicating regularly with the Construction Coordinator
- Drafting any and all set designs to include floor plans, elevations, work notes, etc.
- Distributing all copies and prints to the appropriate department heads, as well as to the Director
- Ordering supplies.

Figure 4.5 Research: colour palette

Figure 4.6 *Coal Miner's Daughter*, Bill Major illustration

Figure 4.7 *Rosemary's Baby*, Bill Major illustration

An Illustrator is the best job in the business.
—Bill Major, Illustrator (*Jaws, The Graduate, Airplane, The Ten Commandments, Rosemary's Baby, Rooster Cogburn*, and more)

The Art Department at Universal Studios used to have a wall near the front offices where dozens of beautiful illustrations were mounted. These represented scenes from famous movies; a night-time moonlit dance under the stars, an interior sweeping staircase in a southern mansion, a battle scene in war, a street in a western town, completely dressed with costumes, furniture and lighting appropriate and accurate to the film.

These illustrations were done to provide a 'concept' of the finished set, and were meant to *convey an impression*. Concept illustrations (or 'set sketches') were done by an **Illustrator** in the Art Department, often drawn and painted or rendered in a day or two, based only on vague, loose information. A good Illustrator could 'fill in' the details with accurate wardrobe, furnishings, lighting, and attitude. Concept sketches help the Art Director/Production Designer to 'sell' their ideas.

Often, the resulting concept illustrations were so successful that stills from the actual movie (filmed nearly a year later) are almost identical!

The artwork brings vision to life, for everyone to see and feel the emotion of the design.
It's a magic all its own, exciting and inspiring.

Figure 4.8 'Dick Tracy/ Gotham', Peg McClellan illustration

Figure 4.9 Sepia Palace concept illustration

Storyboards

Storyboards are a planning tool for filmmakers. They help you visually translate what you see in your head to what the audience sees on the screen. Storyboards, similar to comic books, are composed of sequences of images that visually depict the action and composition of a planned film or television show. These images help each department of a film crew pre-visualize what the final film should look like and determine, among other things, what camera setups to use during production.

In television, **storyboards are rarely used because time is so short in pre-production**. Films (or movies) have a prep time of several months in advance of shooting. Television has mere days or weeks. For this reason, storyboards are considered a luxury in television. Storyboard sequences begin with a **plan** for filming and for blocking the actors and the action. They include the key elements to each shot (i.e. car crashes, breakaway bottles and chairs, etc.) and show relationships in the physical environment and how the camera will cover them. Storyboards are used for several different reasons. One of these reasons is to clarify and choreograph intricate stunt sequences.

From a production viewpoint, the Producers want to know EXACTLY how a stunt or a fight scene will be shot well in advance of actual filming. In a storyboard, production looks for **commitment** to the way a particular scene or sequence will be filmed. Some Directors may resist this because they don't want to be forced to decide ahead of time how they plan to shoot something. Even if you do have a storyboard sequence drawn up, the Director may change it at the last minute; this is all part of the process. Flexibility and preparedness are **essential**, especially when anything unusual or out of the ordinary is being filmed (i.e. children, animals, special effects, etc.). Always be prepared for last-minute changes.

Figure 4.10 *The Birds* storyboard, Harold Michelson, Illustrator

Figure 4.11 *Gone With the Wind* storyboard

Harold Michelson

"The Graduate"

36 - MRS ROBINSON HERE WE ARE ...
YOU GIVE ME A DRINK ...
YOU PUT ON MUSIC

12

36 - "HAVE YOU EVER SEEN ELAINE'S PORTRAIT ?"

257 - MRS. ROBINSON

260 - ELAINE LOOKING UP AT BEN

255 -

Embassy Pictures Corporation

TOP: Figure 4.12 *The Graduate* storyboard credit Harold Michelson

RIGHT: Figure 4.13 Storyboard Artist/ Illustrator Dorothea Holt Redmond

A scene or sequence in a script that justifies the expense of storyboarding incurs additional expenses. These may involve **hiring** outside stunt players and/or a special effects (SPFX) supervisor and crew, **purchasing** additional wardrobe, and **allowing extra time** for hair and make-up to reset if there is blood or mud present. Sometimes, the contents of a storyboard indicate a need for **additional equipment** (such as a **steadicam**, special **crane**, or **dolly**) or **special effects (SPFX)** to achieve the Director's vision. All of these factors cost the production **time** and **money**, and the Producers need to know this well in advance of shooting. Creating a storyboard during pre-production allows you and the Director to think these things through ahead of time so that the appropriate resources can be allotted.

Storyboard Artist

On the rare occasion when a script **does** contain a particularly challenging sequence, a Director or Producer may request the aid of a storyboard to plan out the sequence. In this case, the decision will be made to 'invest' in hiring a **Storyboard Artist** (sometimes known as an Illustrator, although not every Illustrator can or will agree to do storyboards) for a few days. **The Storyboard Artist's job** is to capture and sketch the Director's vision as a way of explaining their vision and literally **staging the action on paper**.

You will want to have the names of a handful of Artists who are talented, pleasant, and diplomatic (sometimes storyboards are kept secret). When hiring a Storyboard Artist, even for a temporary position, they become a reflection of **you** and your standards. You are inviting them onto your team; treat them with the same respect you show everyone in your Art Department. A positive experience for this person will result in further referrals and positive comments about you and help to build your reputation.

Building your reputation, your network, and your base for referrals is how you will acquire future jobs. When you become known for hiring quality people for your team, you will be associated with that level of quality and will be considered for future projects. We will talk more about this in a future module. Remember, take this responsibility seriously and cultivate relationships with **quality talent** you can rely on.

Storyboard Artists meet privately with the Director for about two hours per session. They discuss the scene(s) and brainstorm together, building a sequence that is practical, affordable, and interesting—not cliché. When the Storyboard Artist builds a good relationship with the Director at the outset, it reflects positively on both the Artist and the Production Designer.

A good Storyboard Artist will need to see the **location photos** and any **research** you have for the project in order to accurately draw the sequences and **plot the relationships** correctly on paper, frame by frame. At the end of each session, the Director and Artist will agree on a **deadline** for delivering the rough layouts or finished storyboards. The Artist either draws at a desk somewhere in the Art Department (if you have the room) or works at a home studio.

You should familiarize yourself with how quickly Storyboard Artists can draw and how they prefer to work. Most often, they will have a studio at home and will choose to draw there. They will then either deliver electronic files or hard copies of their work (or both).

BE SURE YOU GET COPIES OF ANY AND ALL STORYBOARDS!

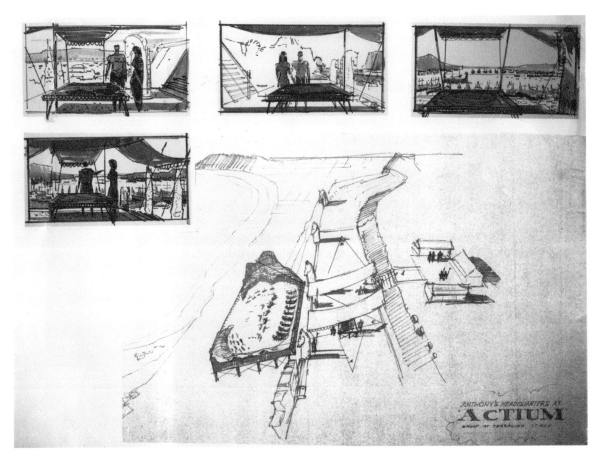

Figure 4.14 Art Department storyboards, *Cleopatra*

You, as the Production Designer, are responsible for the storyboards. You are paying for the Storyboard Artist out of your budget. The Storyboard Artist is a part of your team.

Once approved, the **storyboards are distributed** to a select list (Producer, Director, Cinematographer) or to the entire crew. YOU must be certain that the storyboards are *up to date, properly labelled, and communicate the sequence clearly.*

Be sure to ask your Director if they will need any storyboards **early** in your pre-production, so that you can include this cost in your **budget breakdown**. You MUST know what the Director is planning to do, because this could affect your sets and the shooting schedule. You must be in the loop at all times!

Storyboard Basics (Part 1)

You may, on occasion, need to draw your own storyboards for a sequence, if only to explain the relationships of the actors and action to your sets and locations. In this case, think of the storyboards as a plan to position everything that is necessary in the sequence.

Before you begin to draw your own storyboards or hire a Storyboard Artist, gather some **research** for what needs to be drawn and try to think like a Director. What makes an interesting shot? What is the **composition** of the frame to be? Would a **close-up** or a **long shot** be more effective? Familiarize yourself with some **basic camera moves and industry-standard terminology (included in this module)**.

Storyboards are not about good drawing skills. Stick figures are fine, as long as the **frame is composed accurately** and you show the dynamic of the **intended shot** for the camera. To draw your own storyboards, obtain several pages of paper with standard frames (or panels). You can download or purchase notepads of this storyboard paper at multiple online sources.

Storyboard Basics (Part 2)

It's a good idea to sketch first in pencil within each storyboard frame. This way, you will get a quick 'feel' for the look of your framed sequence, and you can alter accordingly before getting too detailed in the drawing stage. Call this the **rough layout**, or **loose roughs**.

Try to think in terms of composition, regarding the basic concepts of foreground, middle ground, and back ground.

Think like a Director, visualize each shot or frame, and *remember to keep the action/ screen direction consistent; moving in the same direction on the screen.*

A rookie mistake is made when **'crossing the line'** … or, for example, the dog is running LEFT to RIGHT when suddenly the camera **'crosses the line'** and it looks like the dog is running RIGHT TO LEFT.

Some typical storyboard/film abbreviations will come in handy as short cuts to describing the action.

These include but are not limited to:

- **CU (close up) ECU (extreme close up)**
- **2-shot (two in the frame)**
- **OTS (over the shoulder)**
- **MASTER (wide establishing shot)**
- **OOF (out of focus)**
- **RACK FOCUS (snapping from foreground to background image in same frame, blurring the out of focus)**
- **SMASH CUT (jarring cut, usually unexpected and opposite)**
- **TRACKING, PAN, OR DOLLY SHOT (describes the kind of camera movement Director requires).**

Concentrate on highlighting the **main** action in the sequence, breaking it down into a few key frames, and punctuating these frames with **action arrows, energy lines, explosions, or bursts**. (These terms refer to important notations on a storyboard that indicate how things break the frame. Any time you choose to draw outside of your storyboard panel/ frame, you are **'breaking the frame'**. Breaking the frame is done to indicate energy and action, bringing the drawings alive and suggesting motion in the shot.) These notations are also commonly used in comic books and graphic novels.

Sketch of the mission in Vertigo. *Courtesy of Henry Bumstead.*

Storyboard of the bridge scene in Vertigo. *Courtesy of Henry Bumstead.*

Figure 4.15 *Vertigo* storyboards, watercolour. Courtesy of Henry Bumstead

FROM THE DEAD - INT. TOWER & STAIRCASE

Figure 4.16 *Vertigo* storyboards, watercolour. Courtesy of Henry Bumstead

Simplify your drawings and don't worry about your drawing ability. **The storyboard is another type of blueprint; a map for how the action is to be filmed.** It doesn't need to be a great work of art.

In your frames/panels, be certain to use the correct aspect ratio that matches your project. These ratios range from 1:33 to 1:77 to 1:85 and beyond. Speak with your Director to specify the aspect ratio that will be used for the project.

A storyboard is like a second script, only without words. We should be able to 'read' the action at a glance, just by looking at the sequence of sketched panels. Think of the basic visual elements and action that must be represented in each frame.

Blocking in your frames involves **composition**. Composition refers to arranging the contents of a shot to help tell the story. It's what we see of a character (or other subject) in relation to its surroundings. Are you shooting the character's head and shoulders, midsection to head, whole body? Is there a building towering over the character? A road moving away from them? What does the composition tell us about the story? These are the sorts of things the Director considers when lining up and composing a shot.

Try to think like a Director:

- How much empty space (called **negative space**) do you want around the actors' heads?
- Should the angle be from a distance, high and wide, or close up?
- Where should the camera be positioned in order to get the best shot and support the story?
- Would the angle be more interesting shot from the floor or ceiling?
- Should the camera move? Should it **pan** or **dolly**?

Again, try to think like a Director. How would YOU set up the scene for the camera, to make it interesting and effective?

Beware of the trap known as 'talking heads'. This refers to the setups for dialogue (usually in television), where the only thing in the frame is one actor's head, and then the camera cuts to a reverse on another actor's head, so it is as if the heads are answering back or 'talking' to each other. These shots are often **OTS shots**, which refers to a shot on one character's face with the shoulder of the character they are speaking to in the foreground of the same shot. The camera looks over the shoulder of one character at the face of another character.

Always try to find creative ways to frame your shots, but resist the temptation to use a crazy angle just because it may be different. When this happens, the shot usually stands out because it has nothing to do with the **emotional tone** of the scene.

When in doubt, keep it **simple and classic. Always support the character** and the **style of the script**.

Storyboard Basics (Part 3)

Even though storyboards are mainly used as tools for directing, they impart information to many departments and satisfy any questions about how the sequence is to be filmed. (This is another instance of collaboration.) This information will include:

- The number of **camera** setups that will be used
- The type of **camera angles** that will be used
- Any **camera movement**/notes (pan, crane shot, dolly, rack focus, etc.)
- Placement or **spotting of key elements** in the sequence
- **Blocking** and **relationships of actors to doors, windows, props**, etc.
- Possible **lighting** techniques
- Possible **wardrobe** notes (rips, tears, etc.)
- Possible **set dressing** details (chairs, mirrors, etc.).

Think of a comic book; each frame is dramatic. Every frame will have power, impact, and energy suitable to the action.

While a Comic Book Artist may have weeks to sketch and refine a sequence, storyboards for film and television don't need to be completely rendered or 'finished'. Storyboards **merely suggest** the action; the eye fills in the details. Some of the most memorable moments in film are composed simply, thoughtfully, and elegantly.

> You have to talk it out … communication, always!
>
> The Art Department, the scheme, the concept, the money are all related all the way down the line.
>
> That is a healthy thing. Communication.
>
> —John DeCuir, Sr (*Cleopatra, Hello Dolly, The King and I*)

CHAPTER 5

Set Decorating, Props, Wardrobe

We are creating a strong sense of place at every level.

Different tastes and different choices make person senses of style … always ask, WHY make that choice? Which one would your character like? Why?

In this way, Production Designers are like actors.

—Nelson Coates *(Runaway Jury, 50 Shades Darker, Flight, Kiss the Girls)*

Set decorators give definition to the characters. Together, you create a back-story for each character, so that every surface tells a story.

All elements create an environment to inform the actor about where they are; this is also for the AUDIENCE! The audience will SENSE all the backstory!!!

You just have to FEEL it!

—Wynn Thomas *(Hidden Figures, A Beautiful Mind, Inside Man, Do The Right Thing)*

Set Decorator

The Set Decorator is an extension of your Art Department.

You will work hand in hand to create the exact mood and aesthetic statement for the project.

This key position in the Art Department is your closest collaborator.

A good Set Decorator will bring priceless added value to your project. Be certain that you feel comfortable with your choice: hire one you have respect for, and one who shares your design philosophy and approach.

This relationship, when successful, equals MORE than each one of you; together, you create something new, something impossible to bring about separately.

You work together as a team, bringing the sets—and the characters—to life.

The **Set Decorator** (on very large movies there may be multiple Set Decorators or Assistant Decorators), usually has a **lead person** who may work as their assistant.

Figure 5.1 Set Decoration, INT, *Downton Abbey*, downstairs dining room

Figure 5.2 Set Decoration, INT, *Downton Abbey*, library

The Set Decoration Department's duties include:

- Scheduling the crew
- Scheduling furnishings, pick-ups, and deliveries
- Selecting furnishings in advance of shooting with 'hold tags'
- Following up on window treatment orders—design, fabric, manufacturing, and any other custom fabrication
- Obtaining purchase orders from the office
- Measuring for carpeting, blinds, and draperies
- Notifying the lighting department about any lamps, sconces, special lighting, and ceiling fans
- Selecting area rugs, pictures, and accessories; literally everything from rental houses and many other sources
- Balancing petty cash
- Adding any and all of the **critical details** associated with **personalizing a set**.

The Set Decorator's duties vary depending on the shooting location. For example, in New York City they are responsible for floor coverings, tile, glass, all hardware, neon signs, wrought ironwork, and many other things that are usually handled by Construction—in addition to the usual furnishing and wall art in the sets.

There is a common joke; 'in NYC the Set Decorator does "everything"'.
—Tom Duffield (*Lone Survivor, Patriots Day, Hell or High Water, Ed Wood*)

Figure 5.3 Set Decoration. *Grand Budapest Hotel* office set. Production Designer Adam Stockhausen. A dressed set: actor Jeff Goldblum with Madame D's will spread out before him on his desk. The will, like many of the graphic props, was created by lead Graphic Artist, Annie Atkins.

Figure 5.4 Set Decoration, *Grand Budapest Hotel*, reception desk (set still). Frame capture from *Grand Budapest Hotel* showing main lobby reception desk.

Figure 5.5 Set Decoration, *Grand Budapest Hotel*, INT, lobby set, high angle

The following people report to the Set Decorator:

- **Lead person** (assistant)
- **Shopper** (assistant)
- **Swing gang** (also known as set dressers—they move and 'swing' furniture into place)
- ***On-set* dresser** (not to be confused with the *set* dressers), who represents the Set Decorator on set throughout the shoot—these can be valuable allies, as they **photograph the set changes** (which occur through normal shooting and blocking) and they keep the Designer and the Set Decorator informed on current goings-on with the shooting company.

You **must** be able to **clearly articulate** and **communicate** the Director's vision to the Art Department crew and be able to delegate and assign duties with **confidence**. This means knowing the strengths of each individual and working to those strengths to create a smooth operation.

Figure 5.6 Research, *Birdman*, backstage

Figure 5.7 *Wolf Hall*, Cromwell's desk, layered with dressing. Production Designer Pat Campbell. Cromwell's desk is layered with dressing, small props and paperwork. His study was crammed with maps, books and objects collected on his travels.

Props

Props do have to be just right or the whole film looks like a fraud.

The topic of props may be boring to some, but they sure make a difference. Many like props in films when they are the subtle, and sometimes unnoticed, symbols about what is happening in the lives of the characters. But more often than not it is like what Freud says, 'Sometimes a cigar is just a cigar!' All the props needed seem to create tedious work for detail-oriented people who can somehow, thank God, get it just right. As an example, if it is a Catholic movie, the wrong props stand out like a sore thumb!

—Sister Karen Derr

Props

The **Prop Master** is responsible for gathering the many **hand props**—things used in the hands of the actors (for example, the oars in a boat, or a gun).

The basic rule is, 'if an actor touches it, it's a prop'.

All **hand weapons** are **props** and an **Armourer** is usually required to handle, issue, instruct the use of, and maintain the safety of weapons (firearms) on the set. Often, the Prop Master is a qualified Armourer.

Taking firearms to other countries involves a very long permitting process and it's very difficult to get automatic weapons, even shooting blanks, in other countries. The same goes for ammunition.

Money is an unusual prop, as we are not allowed to colour copy it, and the Producers don't want real money on the set, as it sometimes 'grows legs' … so, often a *real* bill is put on the top of each money stack, and it's watched very closely. Or, special money is printed that is very close to real but with the *required differences*, so it cannot be passed in public.

In the instance of **food**, often a Food Stylist is hired to aid the Set Decorator or Prop Master to make a special table or display look amazing.

All props should be approved by the Production Designer for proper colour, style, etc. *before* being presented to the Director.

It is also a courtesy to **allow the lead actors a choice** in the selection of (your pre-viewed options) **jewellery, watches, rings,** or other items they might be wearing or using in the movie, before they are shown to the Director.

Separate prop meetings will need to be arranged for the Prop Master to present options to you, the Production Designer. (There will usually be two or three options to choose from.) **Be sure you allow enough time for this**, as the wrong prop can make or break a shot in the project! Your approved selections will then be presented to the Director for final approval.

The 'aging' of props is essential. You never want brand new rope in an old barn, for example, or a shiny new watering can on a farm; props need to be **aged** to look 'real'. Sometimes it takes an artistic eye to know how much is too much and how much is just right.

Props

Props are important to every project in more ways than you might imagine.

The Property Master (or Prop Master) is head of the Prop Department and is an essential arm of the Art Department and team.

Many things that would *appear* to be **set dressing** or **Wardrobe** will actually fall under the Prop Master's responsibility. These are called 'overlaps', and a good team will work them out between themselves.

A partial list of these will include: wristwatches, specific pieces or items of jewellery, sunglasses, keys, business cards, letter openers, stationery, cigarettes and lighters, newspapers, menus, food and beverages (sometimes tableware and glasses) weapons, ropes, oars and paddles, and so on.

An example of a prop that may appear to overlap with the set dressing team can be found in the Alfred Hitchcock film *Rebecca*, when the main character (Joan Fontaine) breaks a priceless china figurine that was placed on a desk in the morning room. This would be considered a **'breakaway'** **prop**, and several of them would need to be on hand for **multiple** takes (meaning two or three identical figurines would be custom made, just in case they needed to film the breakage scene more than once).

Although the figurine is obviously set dressing, *it becomes a prop* when the actress *touches it* with her hands.

Figure 5.8 Props, bodies and parts, *Gone With the Wind*

Figure 5.9 Vision Board
for *Birdman*

Each prop should be approved by you, as Production Designer, and then by the Director, in that order. You have the vision in your mind of what the Director is looking for, so your input is valuable in selecting *only those props that fit the design brief.*

This will insure a more focused selection to be presented to the Director, eliminating any 'maybes' (a good rule of thumb is to show only three choices, to eliminate confusion).

Figure 5.10 Props, research – *Wolf Hall*

Speciality Design

In the film *Citizen Kane*, many **newspaper mock-ups** were needed; these would all fall under the Props Department.

In the films *Star Wars*, *Blade Runner* or even *Harry Potter*, all **weapons** were considered props, and had to be **custom-designed**, approved, and manufactured well in advance of each scene. This was all the responsibility of the Prop Master (coordinated with the Production Designer).

The Prop Master is an important team member **on set** as well, because many detailed and specific items to a scene are considered 'props', and are needed to outfit the actors or to complete a set before filming can begin.

For example, in a restaurant scene, the tableware, napkins, glasses, food and beverages and even menus (designed and approved by the Production Designer) *are all items touched by the hands*; these would be considered props, <u>unless</u> an agreement has been worked out with the Set Decorator beforehand, which sometimes happens.

It is not uncommon for departments to 'share' the breakdown of responsibilities when these *overlaps* occur.

This is where teamwork and collaboration come into play.

Of course, the **prop cart** or prop truck is always a popular spot during a shoot, because it is a treasure chest of treats; chewing gum, mints, candies, all of the stars' favourite snacks, batteries and often a good brand of Scotch!

(This is in addition to Craft Service cart, which, on a good project, will strive to supply a steady stream of the crew's favourites, to keep all happy and energized.)

Figure 5.11 Props, suitcase of cash

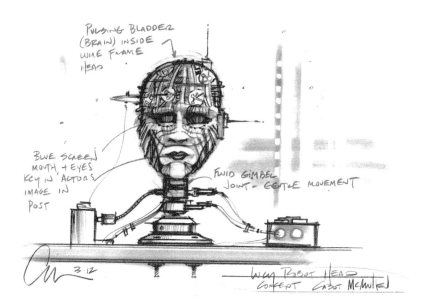

PULSING BLADDER (BRAIN) INSIDE WIRE FRAME HEAD

BLUE SCREEN MOUTH + EYES KEY IN ACTORS IMAGE IN POST

FLUID GIMBEL JOINT - GENTLE MOVEMENT

LUCY ROBOT HEAD CONCEPT CABOT MCMULLEN

Figure 5.12 Custom prop design

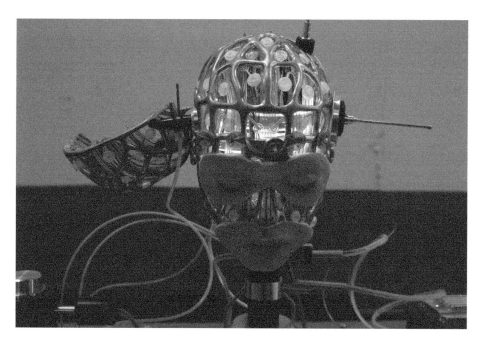

Figure 5.13 Finished custom prop

Figure 5.14 Props, *Imitation Game*, set still, actor at machine

At one time, **Picture Vehicles** were considered part of props.

Today, the transportation department has become part of the creative effort.

Picture cars, **space ships** or **buggies** are a shared responsibility. They say a lot about the characters who drive them and about the period of the story. Sometimes, they are central to the story.

Dr Brown's Delorean in *Back to the Future* is essential to the plot. How it looks, what gadgets it has and what the paint and age are is the Production Designer's responsibility.

Vehicles are another chance to deal closely with Special Effects, Props, Camera, Grips, and of course with the Director, Actors, and Stunts.

Art Director Stephen Dane's drawings of the *Ghostbusters'* modified ambulance are perfect examples of this kind of Art Department input (some excellent reproductions of his drawings are in the March–April 2017 issue of *Perspectives* magazine).

Aging of Props

The 'aging' of props is essential. You never want brand new rope in an old barn, for example, or a shiny new watering can on a farm; props need to be **aged** to look 'real'. Sometimes it takes an artistic eye to know how much is too much and how much is just right.

The **Prop Master** is responsible for gathering the many **'hand props'**; things used in the hands of the actors (like the oars in a boat, or a gun, for example). These props should be approved by the Production Designer (for proper colour, style, etc.) *before* being presented to the Director.

Separate prop meetings will need to be arranged for the Prop Master to present options to the Production Designer (usually 2 or 3 to choose from). <u>Be sure you allow enough time for this</u>, as the wrong prop can make or break a shot in the project!

Your approved selections will then be presented to the Director for final approval.

Location Manager

The **Location Manager** works closely with you (the Production Designer), because you are the one responsible for making sure all locations are suitable for shooting and **restored properly** when the company is finished. (Please see Chapter 3, Pre-Production—Locations and Research.)

Unit Production Manager

The **Unit Production Manager** (UPM) is the one who **oversees all spending and budgets for all departments**. Talk to the UPM if you need to change the schedule—for example, if you need more time to build and dress a set—or if you need more money because the script has been changed and a new set has been added. (The UPM is part of Production, not part of the creative crafts.)

Wardrobe

A Production Designer interacts with every department, some more than others.

The Wardrobe Department brings specific challenges, not only for the obvious requirements of logo designs for company uniforms, proper and accurate insignia used for military and law enforcement, research on period projects, and sometimes, as in a futuristic (*Mad Max, Bladerunner*) or Sci Fi picture, complete design direction for key lead actors' costumes.

Colour palette becomes one of the most important subjects between an Art Department and the Wardrobe Department, not only for seamless cohesiveness and for continuity of design, but for practical reasons as well.

For example, on an early *Mission Impossible* TV episode, a seasoned Art Director needed to create a set that would appear to be in Kenya, Africa, as the script required.

Since the set was to be built on a soundstage in Burbank, CA, his research into materials commonly used in high-end, upscale office interiors was a wood panelling called Zebrawood, specifically found in Africa.

Delighted with his discovery of an economical method to portray 'Africa' without having to rely too much on backings outside of windows or curios placed by the set dressing team, he proceeded to build a fantastic, large, expensive-looking masculine office set.

It was brilliant: the walls were a rich, deep espresso woodgrain, and they were higher than usual, 10' 0" (to suggest wealth).

When the cast came in to shoot the first scene, they were all dressed in expensive chocolate brown suits—and were all African-Americans! Everything blended in with the Zebrawood walls. He had forgotten to collaborate with the Wardrobe Department

Figure 5.15 Logos, patches, uniforms

Figure 5.16 Uniform

regarding the extremely dark wood-panelled walls, where he would also have been told about the cast's ethnicity.

The Cinematographer earned his salary that day, with creative lighting and reflections.

On another show, an 'emergency' set was needed quickly as an office for a lawyer—it was an added scene at the last minute.

Thinking quickly, the Production Designer reused some walls from an earlier set and had them repainted a dark, rich green—the colour of money.

Knowing that the lead actress was a redhead, this PD immediately contacted the Wardrobe team to inform them of the colour for the set. Most redheads photograph brilliantly in green, and, sure enough, an emerald green dress had already been selected for her to wear! She would have blended right into the walls, had the communication not been made (a jacket in another colour was added over the dress).

The point is, never assume your design decisions will not affect other departments; they almost always will.

A good PD will communicate often and regularly, leaving nothing to chance, no details overlooked, with each and every department. This is good management, good practice, good habit—and will always be appreciated.

(Note that communication simply means *collaboration*, as *part of a team*; you are not the designer in charge of Wardrobe! That position belongs to the Costume Designer.)

Wardrobe

Wardrobe will need and appreciate your input on colour (green walls don't work with an actress in a green dress, for example). Any logos, patches, name tags, or uniform designs will affect this department because they need to consider size, style, colour, and scheduling.

A mechanic's uniform will need the logo and name patch **at least** a day before shooting, so that it can be attached. The Art Department designs all logos and patches and is responsible for delivering them to the Wardrobe Department with respect for that department's time and needs. For example, patches need to be aged. Especially in the case of an **old** uniform, the patch may have to be laundered several times. Clothing related to political campaigns, military, schools (which often call for colours and mascots), etc. all require thorough research, discussion, and collaboration.

Finally, remember that a good rule to follow is *don't surprise the Director at the last moment.* Make sure the Director knows what to expect *before* the camera rolls.

CHAPTER 6

Pitching and Presenting

Hitchcock said that if you can't say it in a 3 second clip, you're wasting your time.
—Ted Haworth (*Strangers on a Train, Some Like It Hot, Longest Day, Marty*)

This chapter will cover the basics of **connecting the visuals to a particular theme**. It will discuss the process of **defining the theme, or visual thread**, based on input from the Director and the parameters in the script that relate to the design.

Refining your research is an important part of achieving 'the look'. You might start with a hundred pieces of research and reduce them to the ten that are the most appropriate to the look. 'Less is more' often applies and is a good rule to follow. Paying attention to the many small details (such as a small hand prop, for example) can suddenly become **extremely** important in a close-up. Make it count!

Figure 6.1 Henry Bumstead, Production Designer, pitching to Hitchcock

> Each time you make a presentation to a producer, the visual concept has to be so thorough and so powerful that the need for a production designer is apparent to everyone.
>
> —John DeCuir, Sr, Production Designer (*Cleopatra, Hello Dolly, The King and I*)

The Art of Production Design

> Start with nothingness. When you introduce the first element, you'd better bring in the right element.
>
> —John DeCuir, Sr (*Cleopatra, Hello Dolly, The King and I*)

The approach to designing or finding the look is always the same, no matter the project: you search, research, and **open your mind and senses** to anything and everything you can find that may be pertinent to your project. And then—often when you are not looking for it—you find that *one perfect image* that is absolutely right on every level.

When this happens, you just *know* it's right.

Often, the 'off-times' are when inspiration occurs. Learn to trust this inspiration! Don't overthink this part of the job, because it is more than just facts; **it involves emotions**. This phase should be fun and creative; this is why Production Design is called an **art**.

Every project is different. Every challenge is different. But the process remains the same. You immerse yourself in the written world (the story or **script**), your Director communicates their **emotional point of view** (their **vision**), and *your job is to marry the two appropriately*. Then you allow the magic to happen—the magic of designing **the look**, the magic that is **the power of visuals**.

Designing Emotions

> There is magic in creation.
> The visual world, or 'movie scape' has to look as if it's already there.
>
> —Rick Carter (*Star Wars, Lincoln, Forrest Gump, Avatar, Jurassic Park*)

Figure 6.2 *Vertigo* apartment set sketch

Colours, textures, fabrics, finishes, samples, materials, type fonts—everything that has any-thing to do with style must be considered here. For example, if the setting is woodsy, which types of trees are indigenous to that location? Could trees, woods, leaves, and even tree bark become a theme? Could they become the colour palette?

What you are looking for is *that one bit of inspiration that rings true*—something that excites **all** of your creative sensibilities and makes you think, '**This** is *exactly* what is needed [to suggest the **area**, **the time period**, and **the economic situation** at a glance].'

Colour, pattern, and even a simple sign can accomplish this. The visual can come from a myriad of sources. One thing is certain: the visual will **tell your story without words** through an **emotion**—a response to your visual design and choice of physical elements**.** This, then, becomes **'the look'**.

It will be unique. The look must be interpreted by you, through the Director, and created (not duplicated) specifically by you for this particular project.

And don't overlook the importance of appropriate music to the emotion of the scene! The music is half of what you see.

> You might add your own vocal over the pirate ship; YO-HO, YO-HO, the pirate's life for me! or, there is a shark lurking behind the sunken wreck; 'Ba-dum, Ba-dum'.
> Have fun, act out or sing the scene in your presentation! Your energy will engage everyone and inspire visualization using all of the senses.
> —Norm Newberry (*Ghost Story, Polar Express, The Mask*)

> You have to go through the process of working out your ideas in hundreds of sketches.
> From the minute you read that script those little mental images start coming, and you start to experiment. There'd better be some *feeling*.
> —John DeCuir, Sr (*Cleopatra, Hello Dolly, The King and I*)

Defining a Theme

Defining a theme and aligning your design work with it involves reading the story for the *message*, the *lesson*, or the *moral*; the theme is the **main idea** that can be found throughout the entire story.

Defining the theme is the first thing a Production Designer should do before beginning to design for a project. This is an important first step because the theme will *connect the visuals*, creating a **visual thread** throughout the project. Once you have identified the theme, you can begin to approach the look. Knowing the theme gives you *reference points* to begin research for your **design approach** (also known as your **design brief**).

The **design brief** is a tool for every department—a standard to use for every decision regarding the show.

Themes can be fun because they automatically simplify some of your choices, and a theme, or **visual thread,** will bring what is

Figure 6.3 Production Designer Tom Duffield on set with sketches

important into focus for you. It **simplifies the design process** by providing structure and parameters.

In order to be successful, **your design choices must fit the established theme**. An example of this would be the theme of war and how tragic and destructive it is. Clearly, any design choices involving celebration or happiness would be inappropriate. Design choices following the theme of war would include anything that visually suggests warfare and its accompanying emotions, such as:

- Sadness
- Loneliness
- Hardship
- Destruction
- Despair.

When you are the Production Designer of a project, **be sure to define your theme early— immediately after reading the script**.

First, decide for yourself what you think the theme should be, and then <u>meet with the Director to discuss it</u>.

Be prepared, with visual references and clear examples to support your decision. (If you can relate these visuals to *specific scenes* in the script, you will be extra impressive.) The Director may have a different theme in mind, but they will be interested in your ideas and suggestions all the same. Sometimes an even stronger approach to the look of the project will evolve from this important collaboration.

Production Design is a *collaborative* art. Ideally, you should *define the theme early*, before you begin working on any designs for the project. This will save you time and money and will create an opportunity for you to bond with the Director as you both collaborate to develop and **support the theme with visual choices** throughout the project.

Embrace this crucial step in the process. It is the mark of a true professional.

> As we are visualizing our designs I like to remind our artists that what we are doing will be emotionally enhanced by the music. Half of what we will 'see' is the music.
> —Norm Newberry (*Ghost Story, Polar Express, The Mask*)

Theme

All good stories have a theme. A **theme** is a central idea that guides the action and the characters in the project; it is the underlying and unifying idea of a film. The theme resonates throughout the events and actions of each scene and communicates something in which the writer and filmmakers have deep conviction.

The theme adds depth and meaning to a story because it *addresses the abstract idea beneath the concrete details of plot, action, and character*. This abstract idea is also moulded by the point of view of the screenwriter and Director, and serves to unify the other story elements.

Here is a small list of some basic abstract ideas that have recurred in the themes of literature and films throughout history:

- War
- Revenge
- Mystery
- Love
- Coming of age
- Redemption
- Hope.

A theme should express a universal message. This message comes from a combination of the theme's abstract idea (such as **revenge** or **coming of age**) and the writer's or filmmaker's perspective on it. Since theme also includes the writer/filmmaker's point of view, you could describe a theme as a specific perspective on war, revenge, or hope.

A Guide to Defining 'The Look'—Research

Your Art Department should be the most exciting place for everyone to visit. You should have large, 4' {×} 8' bulletin boards covering the walls, filled with research materials; location photos; wardrobe styles and fabrics; clippings; architectural details; furnishings; colours; paint, wallpaper, and wood finishes; signs and graphics; and even examples of trees and shrubbery. You'll also have images for tone, showing lighting effects, mood, texture, and balance. Always include something a little unusual and surprising, to spark conversation. This is the jumping-off point for your design or 'look'.

Research is one of the most exciting phases of design. You are free to pick and choose anything that speaks to you and seems appropriate, and you have the opportunity to explore unlimited possibilities in this initial stage. Your inspiration might come from a photograph, a letter, a colour combination—even a piece of music! Include everything at this early phase—anything and everything that interests you. Whatever you find for inspiration, make it the focal point of your approach to developing the look. Your design will evolve and grow stronger as you find ways to support the story, the characters, and the Director's vision.

Once you have a **substantial collection** of images and ideas, **editing becomes easy**. Everything that doesn't fit your approach or selected design brief will stand out and be eliminated. Sometimes, you may be torn between two excellent choices. In this case, ask yourself the standard questions of every Production Design brief: **What best serves the story, character, period, locale, and Director's vision?**

The selection should be obvious.

That beautiful landscape photo you love may have to wait for another project … file it away!

Figure 6.4 Period
bedroom illustration,
Gone with the Wind

Figure 6.5 Set illustration
by Bill Major

Illustrater Bill Majors' rendering of a snow-clad setting gives little warning of the menacing events about to take place there. These contrasts can make a horror story that much more vivid.

Figure 6.6 *Gone With the Wind,* staircase sketch

Selling your idea

Energy, confidence, and enthusiasm are what sell.

Remember, time is money, and the executives you will be presenting to don't have a lot of it—it's the old 'elevator pitch' concept, only with a few selected visuals to illustrate your ideas.

Be prepared! Practice your pitch before you get there—you don't want to be 'studied' or formal, but you want to be CLEAR and pitch your most important points and ideas quickly, while you have their attention.

Start with something to grab their attention, something close to the Director's heart, and build to a WOW finish, if you can … it's showmanship, after all. This is your one-man-show!

Don't bring in too much, or anything clumsy—again, hit the main points of the story in an elegant, interesting, and exciting way with VISUALS to express your emotions and impressions.

Tell the STORY through your visuals; let them ask questions about how and so on … of course, you'll be prepared with answers or mention this is just a 'first pass' suggestion.

Focus on THE STORY. Be certain you have selected a theme, a colour palette to support that theme, and visuals to support your approach.

This is your 'dog and pony show'. Plan to bring in energy and arresting, impressive visuals to punctuate the main points of the story.

Don't try to tell the whole story; they've read the script—just hit the salient, MOST IMPORTANT POINTS of interest in the story.

Figure 6.7 *Dr Zhivago* Concept Sketch

Figure 6.8 *Doctor Zhivago* finished set

Everyone does this differently, and has their own style and approach.

John DeCuir, Sr (*Cleopatra*, *Hello Dolly*, *The King and I*) believed in using massive illustrations for impact—of course, he was a brilliant Illustrator, and could easily produce these paintings himself.

Other Production Designers like to present a model of the main set.

This allows everyone to visualize the story and action taking place in a physical environment. Shots and blocking may be discussed, lighting suggestions and solutions may be worked out, and size, scale, colour palette, and props can even be part of the conversation.

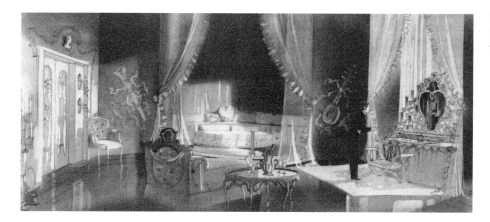

Figure 6.9 Sketch, bedroom/bridal suite, *Top Hat* (1935)

Figure 6.10 Actual finished set, bedroom/bridal suite, *Top Hat* (1935)

Models

Making scale models of sets takes time. A scale model is a physical replica of your set. This is a usually a luxury mainly reserved for films, unless it is a permanent set on a television show.

You may have time to have your Set Designer construct a **foam core model** of a permanent set. This is done by simply gluing down the set floor plan and four

Figure 6.11 *Edward Scissorhands*, foam core castle model

elevations (walls) onto a large sheet of 1/4' white foam core material. These plans and elevations are cut very cleanly so that they fit into the corners neatly when glued together using white glue. The model is then mounted to an appropriate base, such as a 1/2" foam core, balsa wood, or plywood, and any extras (small shrubs, cars, trees, etc.) are added for realism. A model is **always** in perfect scale (1/4", standard) to the build.

Note: It's wise to cut out your window openings **before** the elevations (walls), windows, and door openings are glued in place!

This model is an excellent tool for the entire production team. The **Director** can see the spaces for blocking and planning scenes, the **Cinematographer** can create interesting lighting opportunities, and the **Set Decorator** can see the number and sizes of walls and can make plans for paintings, artwork, wall sconces, and shelves. The model also shows the number and sizes of windows—useful information when planning for curtains, blinds, and window treatments. Some Art Directors/Production Designers may even draw or place scale model furniture in order to help sell the concept and communicate the design to all departments.

A great way to look at a model with the Director is with an upside-down periscope that looks into the model at scale eye level.

The objective (lower) end of the periscope should have an opening that has the proportional format you are using with your camera. The centre of the view should be at the scale of the model about 5' above the floor. (1–1/4" for a 1/4" scale model, etc.) You can make a periscope yourself from cardboard and two small mirrors tilted at a 45° angle.

Virtual computer models are becoming more widespread in use, though they are not to everyone's taste and lack a 'human touch' … technical manipulation mechanically can 'walk' you through the set.

Modelling programs such as Maya and Rhino are popular tools in the digital realm, in addition to Sketch Up, Auto Cad, and so on.

As always, be prepared to sell your ideas *yourself*; physically, with minimum need for props, programs, electricity, etc.—you never know when you may be called on to meet with the Director in a van or on a location somewhere in the desert and he 'just wants to hear your ideas'. You should be able to deliver, with clarity, on the spot, anytime, anyplace.

Models are another mark of a true professional. Many questions concerning the action and filming of the script can easily be resolved by referring to the set model. It enables everyone to visualize the set before it is built. Any problems or red flags can be addressed at this time. This saves money because supplies have not yet been purchased and labour has not yet been expended. It is a good idea to develop the habit of using models whenever possible. They will more than pay for themselves.

Figure 6.12a Set Sketch – *The Imitation Game*

Figure 6.12b Actual Set – *The Imitation Game*

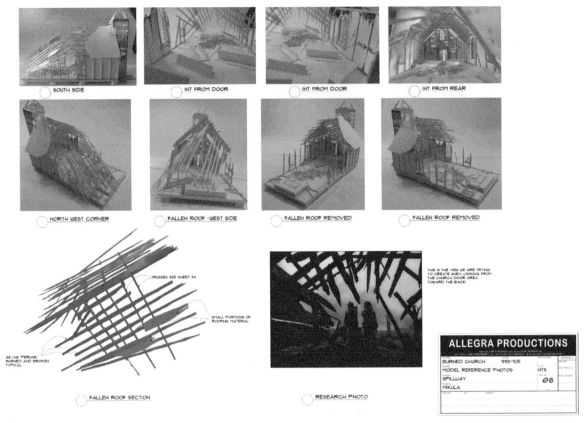

Figure 6.13 *True Detective*, set model, church

Figure 6.14 *True Detective*, set still, church

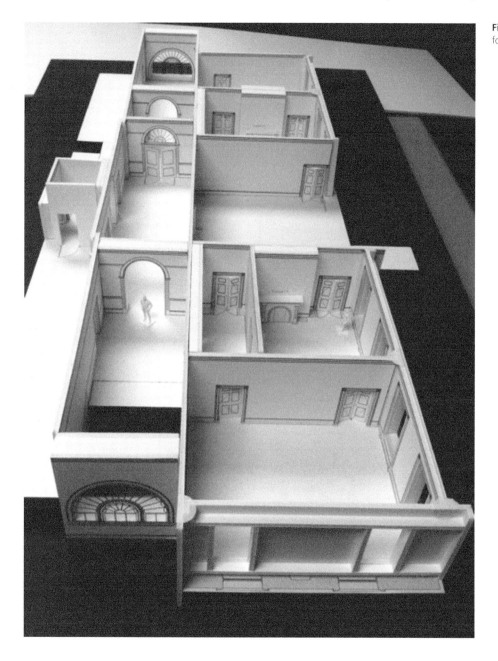

Figure 6.15 *Lincoln*,
foam core set model

Figure 6.16 *Hail, Caesar!*, bar set model

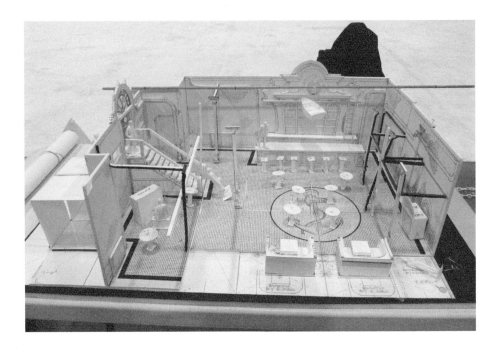

BOTTOM: Figure 6.17 *Hail, Caesar!*, bar set colour guide

DOCKSIDE BAR color study APPROVED v2
set 136
1.9.15

ELEVATION

SCALE: 1/4"=1'-0" (B)

PAINTED as BRASS

WALL COLOR
BM 628 Winchester Sage ?
(CONFIRM color w JG)

WAINSCOTT beadboard
painted brown
(CONFIRM color w JG)

LINOLEUM floor tile

BM 636 Willow Green ?
(CONFIRM color w JG)

APPROVED
REVISED

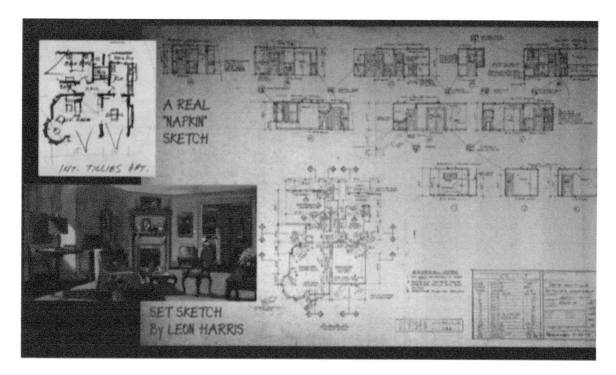

Sometimes, if a model isn't yet prepared and it's early in the pre-production, a Production Designer will bring in loose floor plans, sketches, and even 'napkin' drawings, simply to suggest a direction—for feedback on the approach.

This initial pitch and present meeting may only last 15 minutes, depending on the Director's schedule; use the time well.

Imagine you have to present THE BEST of your ideas, in colour, emotion, tone, and theme—and be certain you have edited just what is necessary, nothing more.

Think of ALL of the senses! Remember that music, a photograph, a suggested smell or taste or sound are all powerful shortcuts to communicating your design approach; use them whenever possible!

A *suggestion* of a nearby train suggests noise and railway grit, a *suggestion* of classical music implies sophistication, a *suggestion* of snowy mountains suggests remote and cold.

Be brief, be excited, be prepared … this is the beginning of your wonderful collaboration of ideas, where inspiration is the spark and where often the end result is unknown until you get there together!

Figure 6.18 *Pete 'n' Tillie*, napkin sketch, illustration and plan/elevations of Tillie's apartment (the result of the cocktail napkin sketch!)

Figure 6.19 SketchUp®
set model

Figure 6.20 Sketch,
plan, storyboards for
presentation (from the
movie *Shane*)

Figure 6.21 *Wolf Hall*, collage/inspiration photos

Figure 6.22 Set Decoration, *Wolf Hall* tapestries based on originals were printed and used to transform sets

Figure 6.23 'Silver Samurai', maquette

Figure 6.24 'Silver Samurai', suit front

Figure 6.25 'Silver Samurai', suit open

CHAPTER 7

Drawing for Film

> Never underestimate the power of a drawing! A good team can build anything from a napkin sketch, as long as scale and/or dimensions are present.
>
> — Chuck Parker, Executive Director, Art Directors Guild

Production Designer Johnny Corso (*Coal Miner's Daughter*, *Breakfast Club*) was known for his beautiful draughtsmanship and lettering as much as for his design work.

In the Universal Studios Art Department everyone liked to comment on the beauty of his plans; they were like works of art, even though they were simply drawn for construction blueprints.

Tom Duffield (*Lone Survivor*, *Patriots Game*, *Ed Wood*) also has a reputation for beautiful draughtsmanship and lettering. Some of his drawings for his early films like *Blade Runner* are collected and treasured as works of art. These are drawn perfectly in scale and fully dimensioned, with his own unique—and tasteful—lettering style.

Hand lettering is becoming a lost art.

Getting Started from the Sketch: Freehand Drawing

> I like to lay out, in some sketchy way, the ground plan of that scene I'm challenged with. Then I have an ardent relationship between the action and the set—they are not just arbitrary movements, but they are definitely moves that are already tied to a set. Then I can be very free and do all kinds of things to augment that.
>
> — Early Art Director

This chapter is about **the value of hand skills**; they don't need a signal, a power source, or any expensive programming software. They are the **gold standard of design** because they (hand drawing skills) communicate clearly and quickly.

Freehand drawing (sketching) skills are **priceless** when it comes to design. They can be crude and simple, yet there is no better way to communicate your vision than by using a few lines on a page. From that point, there is a vision that all can talk about and work from.

This chapter will also cover working drawings for construction, drawn in scale and dimensioned properly for sets and locations.

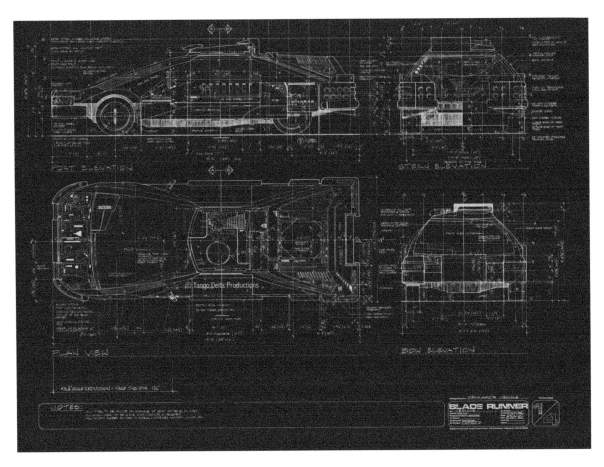

Figure 7.1 *Blade Runner* drawn by Set Designer Tom Duffield

Note: Outside the U.S. most drawings are done to a metric scale, and the material sizing is also a metric.

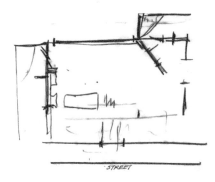

Figure 7.2 Hitchcock, napkin sketch

Napkin Drawings (Part 1)

The ability to **create a drawing quickly and loosely** on paper anywhere, anytime, is a hallmark of any good Production Designer. This becomes extremely important, **especially** when working in television, because time is extremely limited.

It's a good idea to get into the habit of sketching from day one. Start **now**! Carry a sketchbook or notepad with you at all times; the practice will give you confidence.

As a Designer on a project, you will need to become familiar with layouts, proportions, and perspective almost immediately. If you haven't yet had any training, this is the place to start. We will begin with some basics—just enough to cover your initial responsibilities on a project.

Often, you will be on a location scout, in a scouting van, or in a restaurant, grabbing the rare opportunity with your Director to discuss layouts, ideas, spotting of sets, vehicles, stunts, prop suggestions, etc. These spontaneous moments are when ideas come to life on paper through the pen or pencil of the Designer. There's no time for computers, programs, or complicated software. Old-school hand skills will always prevail and impress. Often, this is your only chance to visit the location and gather information; you may be shooting it the next week!

Everyone who has read the script will have some idea of it in their mind. But the moment the Designer puts pen to paper, the entire group focuses on those quick, simple lines, and, for the first time, the story becomes real. **These are called 'napkin' drawings**, because often, they really are done on paper napkins!

All eyes will be on your drawing; 'the way you see it' opens the world of imagination and sparks communication. **One famous Art Director taught himself to draw upside down** because he was asked so many times to sketch something on a napkin at a table while sitting across from the Director!

Napkin Drawings (Part 2)

At this point, don't apologize or make excuses for your drawing skills. The team will notice that **you** have the courage and the confidence to commit your vision to paper. Even though it's just a first pass, it's the beginning of bringing everyone to the same page; this is the starting point of the visual style. You are functioning as the Production Designer; by drawing your ideas, you are taking responsibility for the design of the script. **You** are setting the tone for the look of the project. The true magic of filmmaking begins as you unlock the world of imagination and commit it to paper for all to see.

You'd be surprised at how simple these lines can be. Stick figures are fine; however, a sense of scale and proportion is crucial. For example, if you draw a man bigger than his house, you'll raise a few eyebrows. So begin training yourself now by sketching, sketching, and sketching! Sketch daily in a small sketchbook that you carry with you.

By the way, never, **ever** give away your original drawings! No matter how small or simple, they are the only originals and are irreplaceable. Many designs for *Star Wars* and countless other film projects were sketched out on napkins first.

Always date your drawings; this will prevent confusion when changes or revisions happen. You **must** be up to date when you release the current versions of all designs!

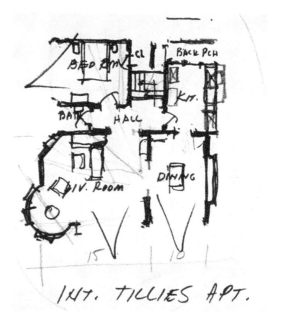

Figure 7.3 Napkin sketch, *Pete 'n' Tillie*, original napkin sketch. Production Designer George Webb found the location in San Francisco, walked across the street to a corner bar, sat down, ordered a beer and sketched this plan on a cocktail napkin for Art Director Norm Newberry and Illustrator Leon Harris to take the next steps.

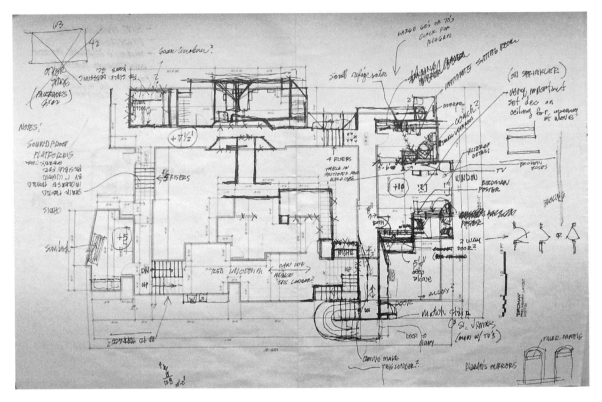

Figure 7.4 Quick sketch,
Birdman layout

Quick Sketch Basics

- Start looking at things in relation to one another: the size of a car, a doorway, a two-story home, a ten-storey office building, etc. Become comfortable with **quick sketching**; don't be afraid. You should use ink because it's easier to read and duplicate.
- Begin with the overall dimensions of the room or space you are considering. Imagine if you had to build it. What questions would you have—how wide? how long? how high? how many windows? where are the doorways? etc. Imagine you are up high, looking down on the space—this is called a **plan**, or a **bird's eye** view.
- **The overall dimensions** of anything are the width and length; adding a ceiling height is a helpful and professional touch for hanging lights and selecting furniture. Always give dimensions in width first, then length or height.
- Each wall is an **elevation**, and should be measured and drawn separately. These elevations are the perpendicular planes of the room. They bring the dimensions of height and volume into play.

- **Grid or graph paper that is divided into 1/4″ squares** is ideal for training your eye to 1/4″ scale, i.e. 1/4″ = 1″. Measure the squares before you buy the paper, because some are not exact and will not be accurate.
- **1/4″ scale** is the standard, unless the larger 1/2″ format is required for more details.
- **Look for openings**, such as doorways, windows, archways, etc.
- Note any **architectural details**, for example, columns, staircases, fireplace, beams, etc.
- Use **callouts** (margin notes with arrows) to draw attention to anything unusual or important.
- **Always do your lettering in ALL CAPS**; it's professional and easy to read.
- **Always sign and date your drawings**, even sketches—you never know when scripts will change or revisions will happen. You **must stay current** and up to date!
- Always put a 6′ figure in an elevation doorway or opening, to indicate scale at a glance.

> **Note:** the reason a **standard lettering style** was developed came from the discipline of Architecture, where it was desired that anyone could take over another person's drawing, if necessary. Using the same lettering style, the change of draughtsman wouldn't be noticeable.

Presentation

It is important to be able to present your quick sketches, plans, and elevations with confidence, pride, and clarity. This is also known as 'pitching'. **A professional is prepared.** Always have properly labelled copies for everyone in the room and do not waste time when presenting your materials.

A **title block** is a draughting term. It is usually placed in the lower right-hand corner of your drawing or sketch and contains the title of the project, the date, the scale (or 'not to scale'), the set number, and your name. This is basic information that should be evident on every design, sketch, or drawing in your Art Department.

Figure 7.5 MGM draughting room, 1951

Figure 7.6 Set Designers in early draughting room

Figure 7.7 All eyes on the sketch, MGM

Figure 7.8 Examples of figures for scale

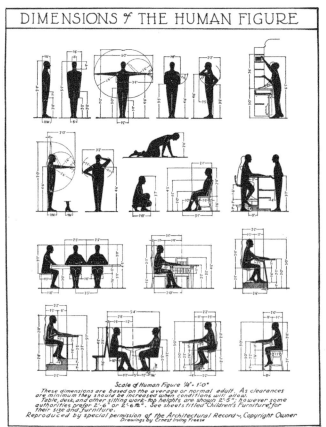

Be clear. You are presenting your concepts to others who do not have your vision, so anticipate any questions and know the answers whenever possible. For example, if the Director asks if the set could be made larger, you need to know if the stage or location will accommodate a larger set, and also whether or not you have the budget for it. Remember the three Cs: **collaboration**, **confidence**, and **communication**.

Presentation skills are a little bit of a selling job. Remember to bring your energy, enthusiasm, and anything else, such as research, photos, colour boards, images—even wardrobe ideas that might inspire the team.

When showing your loose 'roughs' to a Director, be clear that you are **flexible and open** to their input. They are also thinking about camera moves, angles, and actors, as well as addressing your visual ideas.

Less is more. Bring enough visual material to the presentation to 'wow' your audience, but be concise and to the point. Time is money, and the more you communicate your respect for their time, the more you will be seen as a responsible, reliable department head.

Drawing for Television and Film

This segment explains the importance of scale and accuracy in your drawings and set plans, in addition to the necessary research to create your designs. The blueprints provide information to all departments, for example:

- Window measurements for **set decorating**
- Ceiling heights and backings for the **lighting** department
- Breakaway walls for the **grip department**
  - In the United States, the grip department works with camera rigging and lighting, in close collaboration with the camera and electric departments.
  - Breakaway walls are also referred to as 'fly walls' and 'wild walls'. They are walls on a set that can be moved to make space for camera equipment and crew.
- The basic layout for your **Director** to block their scenes and design their shots.

These are just a few examples of how the scale and accuracy of your set plans will affect the production.

All of this begins with **you**, the Production Designer, and your initial measurements. These will become properly draughted blueprints. These floor plans and elevations (once they are approved) can be reduced to fit on an 8–1/2″ {x} 11″ sheet of paper to fit in a Director's notebook or script. You will be surprised at how important these drawings become.

Drawing Set Designs to Scale

Unlike the quick, loose sketching used for the initial inspiration of your design, **scale drawing** is all about **relationships**: showing <u>size</u> and giving **accurate dimensions.**

Blueprints are **drawn to scale, to be built to an exact size**. Accuracy is critical, and no detail should be left out.

Figure 7.9 *Vikings*,
shipwright sketch

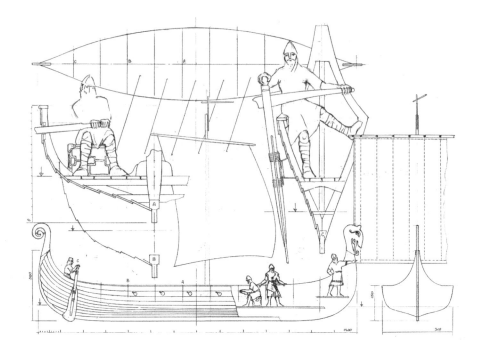

Figure 7.9 *Vikings*,
shipwright sketch

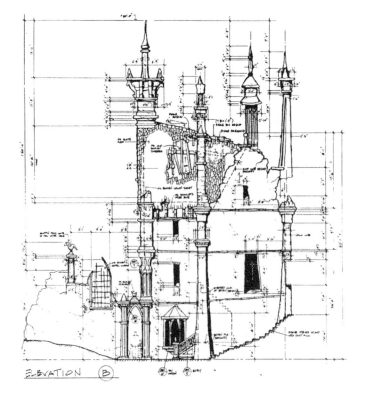

Figure 7.10 *Edward
Scissorhands*, Production
Designer Tom Duffield,
sketch of castle, side view

ELEVATION B

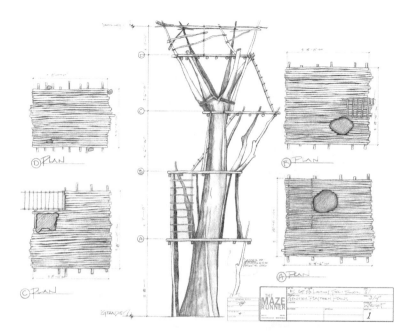

Figure 7.11 *Maze Runner*, hand drawn construction drawing of 'lookout tree', with title block

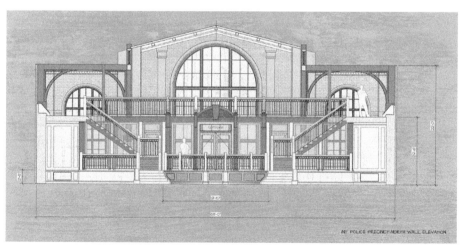

Figure 7.12 *Gotham*, computer elevation, sepia, police station

Now is the time to think and draw to scale. As you train your eye to see relationships and sizes of things (in architecture, furniture, vehicles, etc.), it will soon be automatic for you to find a standard measurement in a room, such as a typical doorway ('3' wide by 6' 8" high'). You will learn to 'eyeball' or estimate measurements until you are able to actually measure the space with a tape measure.

Paper napkin sketches, as preliminary discussion tools, come to life as soon as you introduce scale: 1/4" = 1', or 1/2" = 1' is the industry standard. A **scale drawing** shows accurate relationships between height and width. So if you're drawing in 1/4" = 1' scale, that means a line 1/4" long represents 1' on the set. Likewise, a line 4" long represents 16' on the set.

Figure 7.13 *The Kingdom*, computer action plan

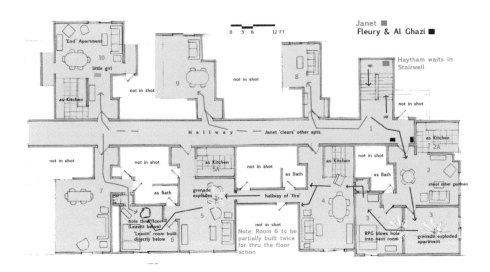

Figure 7.13 *The Kingdom*, computer action plan

On your elevations, it's a good idea to include a simple, stylized human figure (6' tall) as a gauge for size and proportion.

Sometimes, the bare minimum of information is all that is needed to inform the Director of your intentions and to begin the Set Design process. Your Set Designers are **draughtsmen** who are trained to draw the plans of your sets for the construction team to build.

One of the major differences to note between building sets for television and film vs constructing real buildings for the general public is that **nothing is built to code**, meaning that film and TV sets are not constructed to the same safety standards and codes as real buildings.

This is because they are meant to be **temporary structures**, not habitable, and they will be torn down or 'struck' after completion of filming. (The exception, of course, is for a studio backlot addition, which isn't done that often.)

This is liberating, and also challenging, because the designs still need to hold up under practical conditions while filming.

You do not have to be a qualified draughtsman (although it is a great asset if you are), but it is important that you **understand what the draughtsman's job is** and roughly **how much time it should take** to draw up a set of plans.

Today, there are 'digital Set Designers' who never touch a pencil. Using programs like AutoCAD, they develop drawings strictly on the computer. The 'hand skills' of drawing and lettering by hand are slowly (and sadly) becoming a lost art. Much like 'hand-made paper', there is beauty in the natural individual's style.

Most Art Directors and Production Designers come from a background of art, theatre, or architecture.

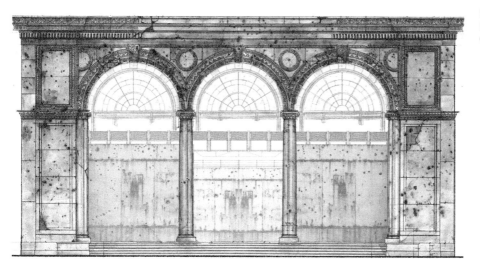

Figure 7.14 *Dawn of the Planet of the Apes*, computer rendering

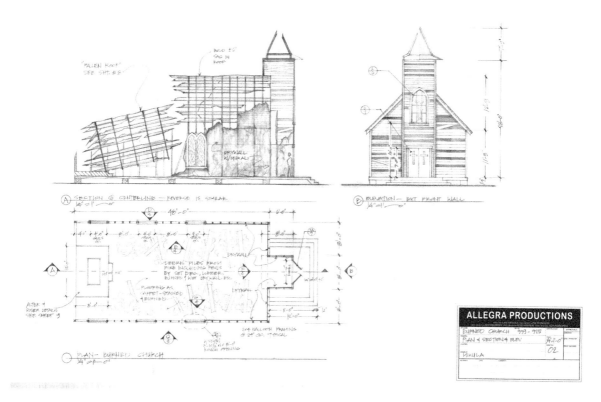

Figure 7.15 *True Detective*, pencil working drawing of burned out church (Note the title block in the lower right hand corner)

Construction Drawings

The Designer uses visuals (environments and settings) to influence the audience's emotions.

When you are ready to progress to the level of scale drawings, you are ready to see your designs become reality.

This means that you must include **all** of the information the construction crew may need on your scale drawings. This should include finishes, materials, styles, colours, etc. When building from your plans, the construction crew may need to consider any special script requirements, such as stunts or actions involving practical effects.

Usually, to save time, these notes are included on your blueprints in a clear, easy-to-read manner, so that questions are answered before they are asked. It is up to **you** to give the build team all the information needed as early as possible. This will help everyone avoid mistakes, saving time and money.

Camera Angles

After you have planned the action in your set and thought about the lighting, it's time to consider **camera angles**. This is the process of selecting a camera angle (usually 35 mm) and then choosing the best spot in which to **place the camera** to shoot the set.

This is not a requirement of Production Design. Early Art Directors did it because they understood the camera, lenses, focal length, and depth of field. Since they had designed the set, they knew how to shoot it to its best advantage.

Production Designers who have background and knowledge still use camera angles to determine the **height of sets and what might be seen in the shot at a location**.

Camera Angles*/Sound Stages

Filming the sets you have designed involves some knowledge and awareness of the camera and camera angles.

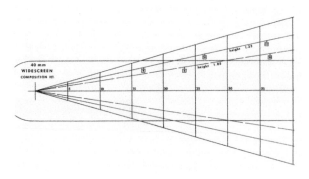

You as the Production Designer know your sets better than anyone else does, because you have designed them. It is to your advantage to learn to use **camera angles**. Especially with alternating Directors on a TV show, the Production Designer is in a position to suggest—as a courtesy—camera angles that will show off the sets to their best advantage. This skill is a tremendous aid to both your Director and your Cinematographer.

Placing a camera angle on the floor plan of your set is a way to indicate the best position for the camera to view your set to its greatest advantage.

Figure 7.16 Camera angle

* Mentioned here as it is *related* to drawing for film.

A camera angle will show you the left- and right-edge of frame (meaning all that will be seen in the shot) and will help to calculate distance.

If there is a staircase, a fireplace, a textured rock wall, or any architectural detail in your set, you may want to feature it, not by putting it at the centre of the frame but by using it elsewhere in the composition. Be creative and think of how you can show the set detail while supporting the story.

Camera angles noted on a floor plan should also give an accurate measure of the **height** of things (walls, ceilings, windows).

A camera angle can be used to determine if you have made the objects at the top of your sets low enough to make it into the frame or if the camera will have to tilt up to capture the detail.

Any Director will be impressed if you take the time to lay a camera angle on your set for them, showing these elements of the shot before they have to move equipment or lights. It shows another level of professionalism.

Continuity is the most important, because it gets down to the shot. Because it's just a series of shots that make a film, without it, we don't have anything. Just building a set isn't enough; it's the shot that counts.

Dream a little, even about opening titles and how they flow into the first scene. Everything has a continuity. It all makes sense.

The development of the picture is important, so I think you should start at the beginning.

— John DeCuir, Sr (*Cleopatra, Hello Dolly, The King and I*)

There is a method called 'projection' which uses a formula that results in an accurate 3D vision of a plan.

Done correctly, this method will produce a completely accurate view of any set from any camera position using any camera angle.

Illustrators used this method to create 'concept sketches' of sets before they were built.

In the early days, the Director and the Cinematographer would come on to a set and find an X on the floor, showing where the camera should go for the best views, angles, and blocking of the scene (according to the Production Designer).

Today, things have changed. The Director and Cinematographer have the final say in where the camera is positioned. You will still be adding that extra touch for your Director by selecting what you believe are the very best positions from which to shoot the action and feature your set.

This is real Production Design: when you know your set and your script so well that you have the **confidence** to guide the Director and the Cinematographer to the exact spot from which they can reliably shoot the scene. All they have to do is light the set and rehearse the actors. Even if they go another way, you've gone on record as knowing your craft—another good habit to develop.

To find the best spot for the camera, lay a camera angle over your floor plan and play around with it. Soon you will see that one or two places show off the set to its best advantage. You may want to favour a doorway, window, fireplace, or staircase.

Figure 7.17 Example of three point perspective drawing by John DeCuir for *Ghostbusters*

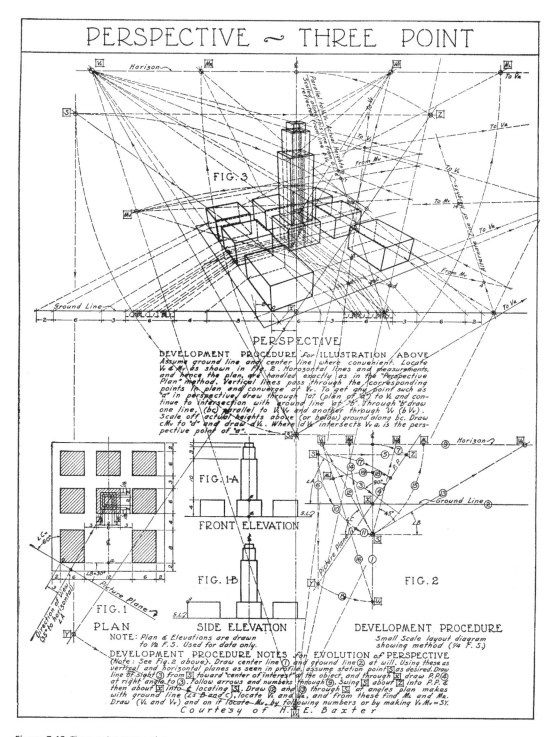

Figure 7.18 Three-point perspective

Stage Plans

You need a space to build your set(s). This may be a stage on a studio lot, a warehouse, or a rented location. Next, you will need the exact measurements of this space so that you can determine how large the sets can be while allowing for a safe and easy flow for the crew, actors, and equipment. Locate the entrances and exits, fire lanes, any columns, etc., and note them on your layout. On major studio lots, these are called **permanent stage plans**.

Once you have your space layout, you can begin to place or **spot** your set in the best possible position. Think about the crew, lights, action, and cameras, and allow for plenty of room around the perimeter. This is to accommodate the cast, members of the hair and make-up team, the prop cart, the craft service/coffee station, any painted or photographic backings, and, of course, 'video village', which is the monitor set up for the Director and the Cinematographer. The shooting schedule will guide you in the placement of your sets, allowing you to 'spot' your sets in shooting order whenever possible. Remember, these schedules are always subject to change.

Stage plans should also show the spotting of the greens and the backings. The **backings should be placed at a distance from windows or doors appropriate to the scale of the image on the backing**. There should also be enough distance in front of and behind backings for lighting.

Consult with the Cinematographer if you have doubts.

Give your initial scale drawings a professional look by **lettering in ALL CAPS**, and adding a **title block** in the lower right-hand corner.

Include all **dimensions (width, height, length)** and any notes or details the builders might need. These notes are known as **callouts**, calling attention to something specific, such as: NOTE! FIREPLACE IS NOT PRACTICAL or KITCHEN CABINETS HAVE DUMMY DOORS. Save any minor or miscellaneous details for section drawings or Full-Size Detail (FSD).

Use softer leads (2B–4B) for your outside wall lines (they should be darker, indicating **solid** walls), and harder leads (F or H) for furniture, lettering, and notes. These lines will be lighter in contrast. This will give your drawing an immediate sense of professionalism by easily differentiating the structure from the details and showing **variations in line quality**.

Remember:

- **Master a simple, 6′ figure** to add to any doorway or elevation for height reference (see Figure 7.8).
- At a glance, your drawings should be **easy to read** and the scale and proportions should be obvious.

As you can see from the examples, your initial scale drawings can be very loose and simple; if they have overall dimensions of all of the walls, they should be enough to get your team started. It's OK to use 1/4″ grid paper, as long as you **indicate that the scale is 1/4″ = 1′ (written as 1/4″ = 1′ 0″)** on the drawings.

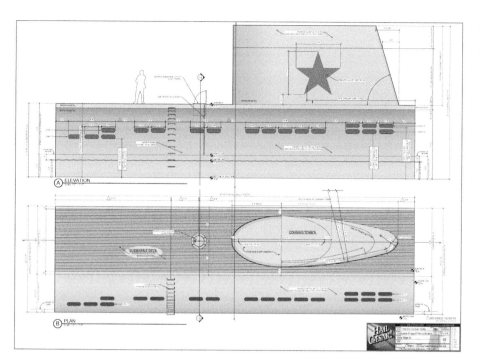

Figure 7.19 Title block and all caps lettering (*Hail, Caesar!* sub)

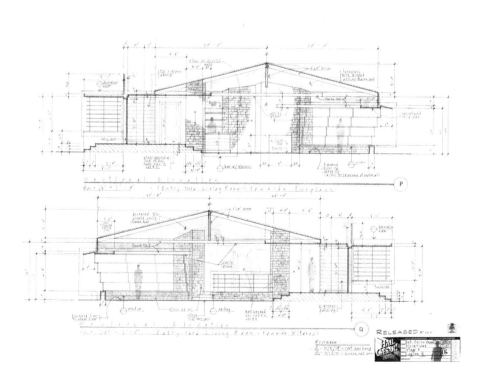

Figure 7.20 Different
leads and line qualities

Figure 7.21 *Kingdom*,
elevations

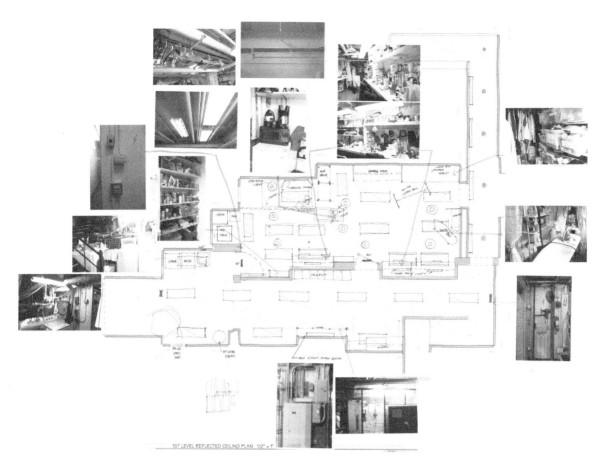

Figure 7.22 *Birdman* collage showing floorplan with research photos for backstage set, by Kevin Thompson

Figure 7.23 *Maze Runner*, drawing for elevator

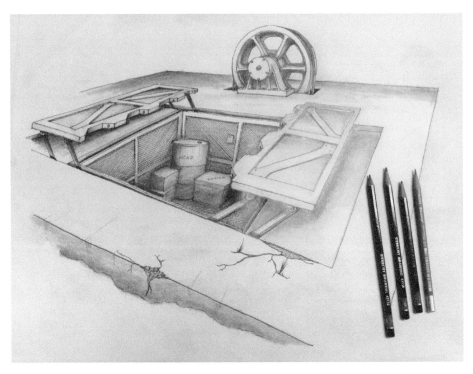

Figure 7.24 *Maze Runner*, elevator on location

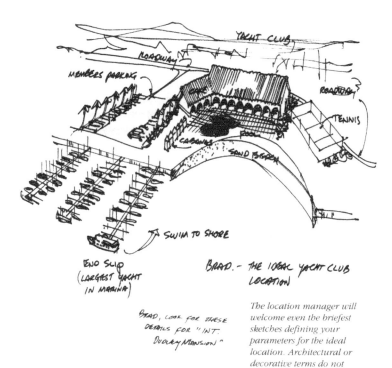

Figure 7.25 Drawing
for film. Loose location
sketch plot plan, yacht
club (set design, excerpt,
Ward Preston)

*The location manager will
welcome even the briefest
sketches defining your
parameters for the ideal
location. Architectural or
decorative terms do not
always bring to mind the
same images. Sketches go a
long way toward eliminating
the semantic confusion.*

Figure 7.26 Stage plan/
set, in progress, *Hail,
Caesar!* bar set

CHAPTER 8

Graphics and Signs

I had to do 170 signs, decals, stencils, etc. for the interior of the helicopter (in Illustrator),
because we had no graphics person. I sent them out to the sign shop to print. The painters
applied them to INT helicopter dashboard.

I drew up the emergency lights (we couldn't get them anywhere); I took a picture, cut
them out of a color xerox and glued them in place.

—Tom Duffield (*Lone Survivor, Patriots Day, Hell or High Water, Ed Wood*)

Viewers take for granted the many directional signs and graphics involved in any production.

In reality, every sign and graphic on camera is there for a purpose, and has been designed and *approved*—especially those in <u>political campaigns, advertising agencies, hospitals, schools, police departments, shipping firms</u>, and so on.

When a script calls for a custom- or specially designed company, the company logo first must be cleared legally for use, then designed and approved by the Director.

Figure 8.1 Dashboard
graphics, *Lone Survivor*

The approved design is translated for use on vehicles, stationery, buildings, even uniforms—and all are strategically placed 'to camera', according to the shot.

When watching a scene where a truck enters a company parking lot, for example, the truck may have a huge logo on the side of the cab or the trailer; the sign on the chain-link fence was also designed, lit, and installed by the Art Department.

These signs are key story points, telling the viewer where we are, etc.

Even the over-used 'AUTHORIZED PERSONNEL ONLY' signs are <u>measured</u> for the location, specified with <u>type font, colour and materials</u>, and then <u>installed</u> by a crew before shooting begins (all under the supervision of the Production Designer).

Often, empty buildings are used as sets and locations, which require new signage and/or possibly covering or hiding existing signs.

An abandoned school might be used as a convent; the old brick architecture works well for the structure, and a strategically placed brass plaque (weathered and aged, of course) spells out the name of the convent and the founding date—signs can make locations work!

Hospitals can be particularly challenging for the graphics team, because of the obvious variety of medical and professional departments, equipment, wards, specialists, supplies, surgeries, wards, emergency room—as well as directories for each wing and parking.

The simplest location or set can often require large amounts of signs and graphics. These would include art galleries, museums, storefronts, main streets in towns, political campaigns, government offices, law enforcement, the circus/amusement parks, state parks and national monuments—even a simple neighbourhood (street names need to be changed and addresses).

Graphics and Signs

This chapter will give an overview of graphics and signs typically required from the Art Department on a motion picture or television show. We will cover the importance of Graphic Design and how to communicate clearly with Graphic Designers. We'll go over strategies for *creating signs, and the necessity of considering lead time (time needed to create, deliver, and install signs) on a motion picture or television production. This module will also explore the interrelatedness of Production Design work with other departments on a production. Finally, this chapter will urge you to develop your awareness of signs in your everyday life in order to discern the messages of signs and discover how you can use them to support stories.*

Graphic Design/Logos

One of the first assignments the Art Department will receive is the request to <u>quickly</u> create a graphic or logo for the show. This main design serves to communicate the show's **identity**.

It will be used on all stationery, show identification, car cards (to be placed on the dashboards of crew members to identify parking), business cards, T-shirts, jackets, etc.

This request comes at your busiest time, and the temptation will be to rush it or to pass it along to an assistant; _resist this temptation!_

This is an important design, one that will live with the show for the entire production. You, the Director, the Producers, cast members, visitors, media, and crew will see it every day. This is also one of your first examples of _who you are as a Designer_; make certain you are proud of everything that comes out of your Art Department!

Try to focus on the <u>essence of the show's story and purpose</u>. Read the logline, which will give you clues to the story's essence. From reading and re-reading the script you will also get a sense of the story's meaning.

A **logline** is a one-sentence, attention-grabbing description of the story. Good loglines include the most fundamental elements of a story—protagonist, antagonist, conflict, a sense of the hook, tone—in an evocative but brief description, so loglines are a great tool to begin discerning the essence of a story.

A **logo** (abbreviation of **logotype**,[1] from Greek: λόγος (logos) 'word' and τύπος (typos) 'imprint') is a graphic mark, emblem, or symbol commonly used by commercial enterprises, organizations and even individuals to aid and promote instant public recognition. Logos are either purely graphic (symbols/icons) or are composed of the name of the organization (a logotype or wordmark).

From road signs to technical schematics, from interoffice memorandums to reference manuals, **Graphic Design** enhances transfer of knowledge and visual messages. Readability and legibility are enhanced by improving the visual presentation and layout of text.

Design can also aid in selling a product or idea through effective visual communication. It is applied to products and elements of company identity like logos, colours, packaging, and text.

Figure 8.2 _All is Lost_, graphic logo, large scale

Once you have a sense of the story's essence and meaning, your graphic logo work can begin.

It is important to have some **working knowledge** of **type fonts**, **styles**, **shapes**, and also **methods of printing**, because *you want to design something practical and within the budget*. You can obtain this knowledge through art classes as well as through your own research and study.

Speed and **ease of reproduction** are important considerations. This is *not* the moment for a three-colour, multi-font, complicated design!

Keep it simple and affordable.

Usually, this show logo will be <u>clear and easy to read from a distance</u>. It is almost always printed in a single colour (with a possible drop shadow or outline). When creating the design, **be very specific about your font size**. Remember to consider upper- and lower-case letters and colour. These are important details to factor into your design.

Try to use the industry standard **Pantone colour system** whenever possible. The reason for this is simple: there are many shades of each colour in the rainbow to be found in every paint department (e.g. sky blue vs cerulean blue, etc.). The Pantone colour system uses a *numeric system* that correlates to inks, papers, shades of vinyls, and even interior paints. The system is used by professional printers everywhere and is universally recognized. Using the Pantone colour system will prevent errors and surprises. When you pick up your sky-blue banner, you want the colour to match your sample **exactly**. **Be very specific in your sign and graphic callouts!**

Scripts do not include graphics, but they will describe or list items such as 'Middlevale Hospital' or 'Acme Printing Co.'

Figure 8.3 *Wild*, national forest signs

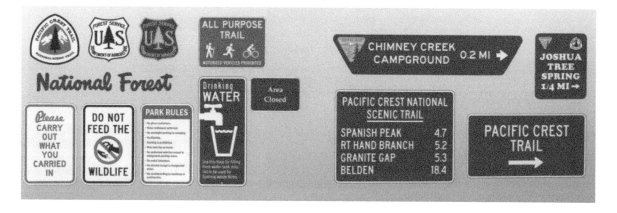

It is the Production Designer's job to design and then to get approval for all graphics:

- Company logos for businesses
- Posters and banners for political campaigns
- Police stations
- Schools

- Hospitals
- Government offices
- Prisons
- Parks, zoos, aquariums, and museums
- Vehicles (taxis, buses, helicopters, police cars, company vans, boats, coast guard, trucks, race cars, airplanes)
- Post office boxes
- Newsstands (which might include creating graphic titles for **all** of the magazines and newspapers on display)
- Shopping malls (including shopping bags)
- Wardrobe patches (for uniforms)
- Props (stationery, book titles, coffee cups/mugs)
- Parking lots and parking structures
- Hallways and elevators
- Commercial kitchens
- Menus for restaurants and cafés.

This list is not exhaustive, but gives you an idea of *the importance of Graphic Design*.

    Graphics may even include <u>background images on a computer screen, mobile phone, or mobile device</u>, as well as <u>dashboard and cockpit labels</u>, especially if there's an **insert shot** of the button being pushed and/or lighting up.

Figure 8.4 *Birdman* theatre and sign

Figure 8.5 Exhibit graphics

Figure 8.6 Museum display graphics

Figure 8.7 Graphics, *Rush*, SketchUp®, illustration/ signs and graphics

Figure 8.8 Poster and
vehicle signs

Figure 8.9 Background
screen image and
graphics

Figure 8.10 Rural Road
Sign

Signs

Signs are a big part of the Production Designer's job.

Every location and major scene in the story *needs to be identified clearly for the audience,* without looking fake or too new.

It is an art in itself to visit a location and to know **exactly** where to spot a sign, or how to cover an existing sign, and to understand exactly which type of sign is **appropriate**. (Neon, for example, would not be appropriate for a library.)

The design must also fit within your budget and time frame for manufacturing and installation.

There is a difference between hand-lettered and machine-lettered graphics and signage; it's the Production Designer's job to know when to use each,

Figure 8.11 Billboard

appropriately. For example, a small-town country fair would not order machine-lettered signs for the pie-eating contest.

Hand-lettered signs are original and will never be the same! They are organic, and have a softer quality.

Machine-lettered signs are repeatable (multiples), have crisp edges and a great font selection.

Study the effects and response you have to all types of signs and graphics you come in contact with: neon has its place and purpose, machine-cut, laser-perfect letters belong in urban businesses and suggest affluence, wooden-router signs invoke nature and state parks.

A note about **bitmap vs vector** graphic application for signage and Graphic Design layout:

- Bitmap deals with manipulating individual pixels (photos, fonts)
- Vector-based graphics deal with movement of objects/combining things (Illustrator).

Signs have character; they have the power of influence and can be subtle, useful threads for your visual theme.

You will be surprised at how **large actual signs** are!

Study them carefully. Don't show up on location with what you thought was a big enough sign and discover it looks like a postage stamp in the environment!

Freeway signs that you always see from a distance can be 14′ tall and 30′ wide. The letters painted on the front of a Western set 'GENERAL STORE' may have to be 6′ tall.

Study your research, try to figure out the scale of things by assuming the people next to signs in the photos are about 6′ tall. The height of one storey of a tall building might be 10′ to 13′ tall.

Signage can help sell your location; '*Capital Cleaners*' or '*Cable Car Grocery*' can indicate you are in Washington, DC, or San Francisco.

You can be cleverer than these examples … you get the idea.

Figure 8.12 Posters,
Gone Girl

Figure 8.13 *Broken City*,
campaign headquarters,
graphics

Figure 8.14 *The Kingdom*, Saudi freeway and exit signs

Figure 8.15 *Hacksaw Ridge*, movie poster

As an example, let's say your script calls for a character who is running for the political office of governor. This means, in addition to all of your other duties, you must **design a campaign** for this character and **look for places to utilize the designs within the script**.

You might start with the **colours** of the campaign. Researching other campaigns will show you what has been done before. Don't copy—always strive to be original.

Next, *find out the specifics in the script* of **what kind** and **how often** the signs and logos will be used. This will tell you **how** to design. Will there be **banners? Posters? Bumper stickers?** Will you need lapel **buttons, billboards, or bus signs?** Will *photographs* be needed?

If you need to create photographs, <u>this will involve a special photo shoot with the actor,</u> *involving wardrobe, hair and make-up, lighting, a photographer, photographic backings, etc.*

This is just one example of how your designs will affect **every** department, from lighting, to wardrobe, to transportation. Think about how the Art Department must integrate with the rest of the production.

Good communication and collaboration will save time and prevent mistakes.

Figure 8.16 Presidential seal, TV graphic, with call outs and dimensions

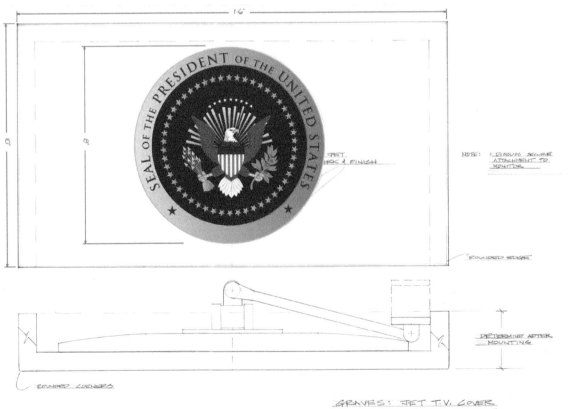

Logos and other designs should be **easy to read**. *Choosing an appropriate lettering style (font)* is <u>extremely important</u>. A rookie mistake you should avoid is making the design too complex to communicate the message clearly at a glance. Think of iconic logos we all know: Coke, Apple, Nike, etc. They work because they are instantly recognizable. They are **strong**, **clear**, and simple, yet interesting.

Your challenge is to design graphics and signs that are **pleasing to the eye**, **appropriate to the subject**, and **communicate the intended message within seconds**. It may be helpful for you to close one eye to check your finished design; **this** is what the camera sees! This simple trick will force you to **simplify** when designing for the single lens of the camera.

Here's one final tip for making your signs look authentic:

One of the hardest things to do is to make a new sign look old, or to make a **manufactured sign look handmade**. A trained **signwriter** will find this task nearly impossible! They simply **cannot** make their work appear less than perfect; they are professionals. Even their 'mistakes' look professional!

A solution to this, as told by an early Universal Studios signwriter, is this:

> If you want posters or signs to look homemade and hand-drawn, don't ask a <u>professional</u>. Ask someone in your family to do it, and **to do their very best**. They will come out looking exactly as if an amateur did them. Works every time.
>
> Quote paraphrased by Ward Preston in his book *What an Art Director Does* (1994, p. 174) *'Signs of Protest Are Best Done by Amateurs'* (author's emphasis added)

Figure 8.17 Amateur protest signs

Graphic Designers and Communication

Graphic Design is not easy, which is why Graphic Designers are often hired as outside contractors. Military, police, hospital, fantasy, and period films and television shows, as well as those set in other countries, present an obvious need for **massive graphics** and **signs** of all sizes. A good **Graphic Designer** who is **fast** and **reliable** is a **valuable team member** to have in your Art Department.

The budget will not always allow you the luxury of hiring someone just to design your signs and graphics. If that is the case, you will have to do it yourself. Or, when hiring, you may be lucky to find an Art Director or a Set Designer who is skilled in this area. Not all budgets will allow for the hiring of a specific position for a Graphic Designer in the Art Department. The Production Designer is allowed to recommend Art Directors and Set Designers they would like to hire, and if they are available, to offer them the job.

Of course, as the head of the Art Department, **you** should cultivate the good habits of basic Graphic Design yourself. This makes you more valuable to the team and will give you the confidence to request any type of design, any time, in any circumstance.

Even if you do have a graphics person, you will have to communicate what you want **in writing** (to protect yourself and your design, and to ensure you get EXACTLY what you have ordered).

Some basic items you might need to communicate to a Graphic Designer (in writing) are listed here:

- SIZE = scale
- STYLE = traditional, modern, serious, playful, etc.
- FONT = lettering style
- COLOUR = the universally accepted Pantone colour system. You may want to get a fan book of their colours for your next job; this will ensure consistency of any colour you call out. To find out more about Pantone colours, please see, for example, www.**pantone**.com/ **pantone**-numbering-**explained**,   www.**color**guides.net/**pantone**.html,   **https://en. wikipedia.org/wiki/Pantone** for some useful online Pantone resources.
- PURPOSE = What is the purpose of the sign? Is it to show direction? Will it be needed to illuminate an entrance?

Sign Installation

When designing your signs, it's important to consider how and where the signs will be placed, mounted, hung, or attached.

Often, one of your greatest sign challenges will be to cover or obscure existing signs on buildings or locations.

Installation (and removal when filming is completed) will always play a role in how and what you design when it comes to signs and graphics, especially on locations.

How will the sign be installed? Will it be mounted on brick? Should it be made of vinyl letters for a glass storefront? Is it to be carved out of wood? If so, will it need to be ACTUAL wood, or AS WOOD (lightweight simulation)?

Should the sign in a bar be neon? If so, dimmers will be needed and a special crew to install the fragile glass tubes.

Will your sign be attached to a vehicle? Should it be magnetic or vinyl letters?

Is it a banner? If so, what material and how will it hang—vertically, or horizontally?

Will there be any graphics *on a screen* (television, computer monitor, phone, iPad, etc.) in the background (often called 'ghost images', which must be added to your budget and timeframe)? Will there be a *fictional TV logo* (as on microphones, cameras, camera trucks, etc.)?

When writing out a description of a sign or a graphic, try to imagine that **you** must create the sign or graphic yourself. How big does it need to be? Include **exact dimensions: height, width, and depth.** What **materials** do you need?

How will the sign be attached, or presented? Will you need additional posts, supports, or matching finishes to the location?

Answering these questions yourself gives you the outline of a proper sign shop order. Here is a template guide for a sign shop order:

PROJECT:
DATE:
YOUR CONTACT INFORMATION:
DATE NEEDED (delivery):
SPECIFICS:

- **TYPE OF SIGN (banner, magnetic, prismatic [raised] letters, etc.)**
  Note: Neon signs involve the use of transformers and dimmers, which affect the electrical department. **Be certain** to notify the gaffer whenever neon will be used! The transformers and dimmers often create a buzz or humming noise that affects the **sound engineer on set**. They, too, will need to be made aware of what to expect, so that adjustments can be made accordingly. As always, **collaboration** and **communication** are crucial to successful Production Design.

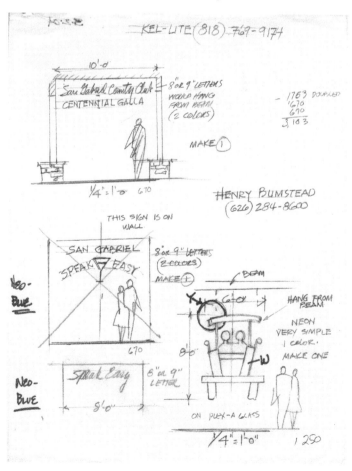

Figure 8.18 Freehand sign order (neon), Henry Bumstead

- **SIZE**
- **NUMBER OF SIGNS**
- **FONT(S)**
- **COLOUR(S)**
- **INSTALLATION AND TOOLS REQUIRED (LOCATION OR STAGE SET)**
- **STRIKE DATE (removal)**

Figure 8.19 Installing dashboard graphics, *Lone Survivor*

Lead Time

It's important, also, to remember the **lead time**. This refers to the amount of time it will take **in advance** to **design, manufacture**, and **install** your signs and/or graphics (or anything else a production needs) on your set or location. *It's essential to make sure you have enough lead time before production begins.* For example, a large hospital may need so many signs and graphics that it could take a print shop up to a week to complete the order, plus another day or two to install the signs and graphics. That means you need a lead time of at least nine days.

Supervision at the installation stage is **necessary**, so you must plan your time accordingly. You or a knowledgeable assistant must be there to **spot (determine)** the *exact height and location* of your signs. You cannot expect anyone to read your mind!

The Power of Signs

Develop the habit of noticing signs in your daily life and surroundings. Become aware of unique and unusual signs, especially signs that are handmade, old, aged, etc.

An example would be: Antique Western Lettering, hand-carved into an aged plank of barn wood symbolizes a **rustic, country, casual** message as opposed to something **clean,**

Figure 8.20 *Wild*, cabin location, signs

modern, and **contemporary**. The point is, the STYLE of signs and graphics, including type fonts, colours and materials affect the message (meaning or purpose of the sign) without even reading the words.

A well-designed sign will be appropriate to the scene and will reflect the tone and character of whatever it is representing.

As you can see, signs and graphics are more than just letters on a poster. They telegraph your message to the audience the way that a bull's-eye does on a target. Never underestimate the power of your signs. They may seem incidental, but they are important clues to the story, the characters, and the locale.

Figure 8.21 EXT Location, Richard Graves Library Sign

CHAPTER 9

Studios, Stages, and Set Construction

*I believe if you're going to do your finest dramatic job, you're going to have to acquire a stage
and work under <u>controlled conditions.</u>*

Nature has great beauty, but it isn't always controllable.

—John Decuir, Sr (*Cleopatra, Hello Dolly, The King and I*)

Production Designer Dick Sylbert once said, 'I never film on backlots, because I don't believe
in using "icons" …'

He preferred to <u>personally</u> find and scout locations for his movies, because he believed it
was the job of the Production Designer to select and create the film's environment, and that
this was part of the art of designing the picture.

He learned this attitude from working with Wm. Cameron Menzies. Menzies was so
completely involved in every aspect of designing Gone *With the Wind*; storyboarding and
even filming some of the scenes himself, David Selznik decided to *create* a new job title,
because the traditional 'Art Director' simply wasn't enough. The title 'Production Designer'
was created for Wm Cameron Menzies as a reward for years of his complete and total
involvement in every aspect of the visual style of the film.

To this day, Production Designer is considered a special job title.

This chapter covers designing for the camera, and the specific requirements of
filming on stages. Designing for the camera simply means closing one eye. This is what
the camera sees. Much of the small detail is lost because you are using one lens instead
of two.

The 'broad strokes' of the overall design need to be clear and strongly recognizable.

Knowing how to use the stages to the best advantage of the entire shooting company is
the mark of a truly experienced and considerate Production Designer.

Sound Stages

You will need a place to build your sets.

This can range from an empty warehouse to an unused office complex, or, if you're lucky,
a motion picture studio lot.

All major studios have what are called '**permanent stage plans**', which are useful blueprint drawings showing the layout, size, and location of each stage.

Figure 9.1 1940's EXT, sound stage, Warner Bros

These are used to keep track of what is built on what stage for scheduling the use of the stages on the lot.

Usually, on a television series, the production company will rent one or two of these empty sound stages for your show; these are yours until the show wraps, and will become the home of your Construction Coordinator and their crew.

They will immediately set up shop. This consists of a small office (locked), a land-line phone, a show calendar and shooting schedule, a coffee pot and water cooler, filing cabinet, and a desk. This office will also need an Internet connection.

Just outside this office will be a simple table called a '**plan bench**', where your set designs and blueprints are laid out for all to see and to refer to as they are being built.

Your Construction Coordinator is the Production Designer's right arm, and you should make a **habit of visiting them first thing in the morning, every day as early as possible**. Construction crews start at 6:00 am and leave at 2:30 pm, unless you need them to work overtime.

Typical workdays are 8-, 10-, and 12-hour days, usually starting at 6 am to 2:30 pm, 4:40 pm, and 6:00 pm.

Figure 9.2 Stage set, *Laura*

You **never** want to hold up a crew because they are waiting for answers or directions from you!

Try to have an agreement between your Coordinator and your Art Department to check in daily before they leave for the night. This will help to avoid any 'waiting' on their part when they come in for work at 6:00 am the following morning.

There will ALWAYS be questions about your sets: questions about scheduling, costs, finishes, and so on. You will need to stay on top of the progress of the build because your **sets must be ready IN ADVANCE** of the scheduled shooting date.

Once built, a set must be painted or papered, dressed and lit. All of this needs to happen early enough to be ready BEFORE rehearsals and shooting can begin.

On a weekly television series, you will have less than one week from script to shoot … so time becomes the most important commodity. On a feature film, the time from script to shoot is usually a few weeks to a few months, sometimes even a year.

Stage Plans

When you know where your stages (or warehouses) are, the first thing you need will be up-to-date **stage plans**. These show the accurate dimensions of the space, including width, length, and height. Restrooms, plumbing, control panels, and electrical supply should all be accurately marked.

Figure 9.3 INT, Paramount Studio sound stage (1930)

Figure 9.4 Water tank under stage floor

Be certain these plans are up to date; you don't want to design a large set over a pit in the floor that was never indicated on the plan (it has happened).

If no such plans are available, you will need to send a Set Designer (draughtsman) to **measure and draw up the area**.

<u>**You cannot design accurately without this key information!**</u>

Fire lanes should be clearly marked on the stage plans, and painted on the actual stage floor in yellow, 4' from stage walls.

<u>These lines are for the safety of cast and crew and are to be kept clear at all times</u>. Nothing should block these lanes in any way. Even a broom leaning up against the wall could result in a fine from the Fire Marshall.

Figure 9.5 *The Ring*, sets under construction, Sony Studios

Once your sets have been designed and drawn in scale by the Set Designer, they will need to be 'spotted', or **specifically positioned on the stage floor**. Do this together with your Construction Coordinator and have them tape it off on the stage floor before anything is built. This will ensure that your sets will fit, allowing plenty of space for any backings, stage braces, greens, etc. around them.

When spotting your sets, think about every detail as though you are the Director, shooting the scenes yourself:

- What are the **key scenes**?
- Where will the **action** be?
- **How many pages/days** will be filmed in this set?
  - Will they be shooting here a day, a week, or longer?
- Will they be **day**, **night**, **or both**?
- **Will you need backings?**
  - If so, how much 'throw' (distance) from the backing to the set is needed? Allow for bracing, hanging, and special lighting rigs; a big lamp can't be right up on the set. Height above the set is also a requirement, as all DPs light from above to some degree (see Backings, Module 13 for additional information)
- Will you need **greens** (plants, shrubs, trees, branches, flowers)?
- **How many walls are 'wild'** and which ones?
  - This will affect your placement of the set, for easy removal of wild walls or flats
- Do you need room to build additional 'swing' sets on this stage?
  - A 'swing' set is a minor, smaller set needed occasionally for a scene or two. It 'swings' in for filming and 'swings' out to be stored for future use.
- Make sure you have left enough room on the stage for the shooting company.
- Also consider equipment outside the stage walls, i.e. air conditioning equipment, camera, electrical and grip equipment, wardrobe trailers and dressing rooms, catering trucks, etc.

○ Camera angles noted on a floor plan should also give an accurate measure of the height of things (walls, ceilings, windows - see Chapter 7).

○ A camera angle can be used to determine if you have made the objects at the top of your sets low enough to make it into the frame or if the camera will have to tilt up to capture the detail. (NN)

Figure 9.7 Rope set, stage, Hitchcock

Figure 9.8 *She* (1936), scale and scope of stage set

Figure 9.9 *Lone Survivor*, gear up set, all wild walls

Figure 9.10 INT, plane set on stage

Figure 9.11 Stage set, dancers, *Hail, Caesar!*

Always allow for easy access for the crew, <u>especially set decorating and lighting</u>, **to enter and exit your set with ease** and to do their jobs efficiently. Place the open end of the set (also known as 'the 4th wall') <u>so that it faces the large stage doors for ease of loading and unloading of equipment, lights, and furniture</u>.

Figure 9.12 Stage set, light beds, house

Figure 9.13 Stage set, nose cone

Easy access means that you will **usually position the set on the stage with the 'open wall' pulled out**. This wall should be standing by, ready to be put back in place for reverses and coverage shots.

Be sure to position your set underneath existing overhead lighting grids (also known as **green beds**) to accommodate the Cinematographer and to allow their crew to take advantage of the grids for their lighting needs.(Green beds are a studio luxury these days, but they are all unique and almost always need to be redone for each new set.)

This shows consideration and professionalism.

With all of the **seams** and the **corners** between 'wild' walls and the pulling of set walls for any variety of camera angles, it is good to plan ahead for possible chips or noticeable 'breaks' in walls. 'Pre-breaking' the seams and having the standby painter ready to repair them as necessary is the usual routine. 'Taping' seams and joints (with pre-painted, extra-wide masking tape) is mostly for TV.

A simple and effective way to cover these seams and/or chips, is to have <u>pre-painted strips of wide masking tape</u> on hand. These strips can cover a multitude of sins and will allow filming to progress without waiting for paint to be touched up and to dry …

Figure 9.14 Bram Stoker's Dracula

Figure 9.15 Spotting sets, crew considerations

Figure 9.16 The Ring, sets under construction, Sony Studios

Standard Terminology

There is a rhythm to shooting a scene that makes sense, which you will learn by watching the Director. Here is a **partial list of industry standard terminology to be aware of:**

MASTER, TWO-SHOT, OTS (over the shoulder), CU (CLOSE-UP), ECU (extreme close-up), MONTAGE (a collection of images/scenes collaged together), and MOS (mit out sound; no sound recorded—attributed to Director Eric Von Stroheim).

NEW SET UP: This means the camera will move to a new position. Therefore, a wall may need to be pulled out or put back into place. Your Construction Coordinator will have already met with the grip crew and discussed which walls are built to be **'wild'** (which means to come apart easily with double-headed nails), and so on.

COMPANY MOVE: means the entire filming company (including talent) packs up and moves to another location. They then park, unload, and unpack everything they will need to **prep** the new location.

Figure 9.17 Stage set, *There Goes My Girl* (1937)

Company moves are costly because they take time. No matter how close in distance they are, the entire crew must stop work, pack up, drive to the new location and find a place to park, then unpack again and re-position and re-acquaint themselves with the new location. This is a very time-consuming process.

When there is a company move, the rhythm of the crew is broken. It takes a while for the group to settle down again and get back to business.

For these reasons, **company moves** are considered undesirable unless absolutely necessary.

Once the camera rolls on the first shot, the Production Designer is allowed to leave. The Production Designer will then go to check progress on the next set under construction, and/or location, check with the Art Director, the Production Office and so on.

Television Considerations

Series television is not for the faint of heart; from the minute you receive the script for Episode #1, you are off and running and you won't stop until about a week or two after the entire season wraps.

Your first script has a Director, sets, and locations. The most important sets will be the **'permanent sets'**, which deserve the greater part of your time and budget. These are your big sets for the series, which will be used in every episode.

In addition to these, the major characters will have homes, coffee shops, or 'swing' sets that will be written into future episodes on a regular basis.

While you are prepping and shooting **episode one**, you will receive a script for **episode two** (with a new Director), which will have new locations, sets, etc. Your new Director will be eager to meet and discuss their special take on his show. You 'steal' time from episode one for this and juggle both episodes/Directors at once. This balancing act continues throughout the series.

Your Art Director or Construction Coordinator will be on call to manage the sets that are currently being used for shooting.

The Production Designer is handling **production meetings** with the whole team: Art Department, Set Decorator, Props, and Construction. You are keeping up with schedule changes. You are dealing with 'surprise' **cover sets, inserts, re-shoots, location issues**, and so on.

Communication is essential. It should become second nature to you and your entire team. Everyone must be on the same page at the same time! This is called 'running a tight ship'. Because everyone is collaborating and communicating regularly, communication pays off when one small thing might be accidentally overlooked and another member of the team has it covered.

You will soon develop a system for juggling all of the various duties, departments, and details on a daily basis. In a short while, with the help of good habits, you will have trained your crew and established a system of staying ahead of the shooting company, i.e. having your sets camera-ready before the shooting crew arrives to for filming.

Studio Stage Considerations

To review, some of the details to be considered when using studio stages include:

- 'Spotting' a set under existing overhead lighting grids, for ease and convenience of the lighting department
- Positioning a set on the stage with plenty of room around its perimeter for backings and stage braces
- Accommodating hair and make-up tables
- Considering the sound engineer's area, close to the set and actors
- Allowing an area for the prop cart (these vary in size, from a small cart to a small trailer)
- Allowing for craft services (food) to set up—at least two large tables, beverage coolers, and miscellaneous appliances such as a microwave, toaster oven, and coffee service in a practical and convenient location (not too close to filming)
- Positioning the **'open wall'** of the set closest to the stage door, for ease of equipment and furniture loading
- Considering seating area for **'video village'** for Directors' chairs, monitors on stands and headphones
- Chairs and seating area for performers.

Greens

The **Greens Department** covers everything you may need for a set's garden, gazebo, pool area, park, or outdoor space. This includes artificial rocks (made of fibreglass), faux concrete garden benches, planters and planter boxes, trees, shrubs, vines, trellises, 'wild' branches (often stapled to your set walls' outside windows for shadow effects), garden ornaments, baskets, stone urns, statuary, arbours, hedges, silk flowers, and sometimes even different types of fencing. The trees range from palm trees to elm, oak, and maple. The Greens Department even has a variety of tree stumps, driftwood, tumbleweeds, and cacti.

This is a fun department, and you shouldn't overlook it as a source of design inspiration. Often, you may not even know what you need until you see it among the many rows of items available.

Usually, you will schedule a visit to the **nursery** (for plants) or Greens Department with a specific guide. Your guide will drive you in a golf cart through the rows of plants, trees, and bushes. They will ask you what kinds of plants or other items you're looking for, how many you need, and in what sizes. Your guide will try to gather from you some basic information about the set and the project.

Figure 9.18 *Wild*, greens list

Figure 9.19 *Maze Runner*, greens applied to set

Figure 9.20 *Dawn of the Planet of the Apes*, set dressed with greens

Be sure you are prepared! Bring a layout (a floor plan or plot plan) of your set area (always to scale); this will be extremely helpful, not only for selecting and filling, but for notes on spotting what goes where. Leave a plan with your guide to attach to your order. This will save time on delivery when placing items in the set.

Once you have discussed the project with the Greens Department, they may have better ideas and/or alternate suggestions for you. These people are experts. Always listen with an open mind, and take their advice. It is their job to know which plants grow where. They also know their inventory and may be aware of some treasure you haven't yet seen.

Greens on stage can hide the edges or bottoms of a backing. Make sure you have matching greens on the location or backlot set.

When you are considering the 'softscape', don't forget the 'hardscape'; planter boxes, sidewalks, patios, or benches that may be integral to the greenery.

Occasionally, you will have conditions come up that have no explanation. For example, on one set the production team decided to dress a courtyard area with wisteria for its beautiful lavender flower clusters and suggestion of romance. The set looked beautiful in person, but on camera, **the lavender flowers photographed as grey!** Even the **greens person** couldn't explain this. After several tries of spraying the flowers different **shades** of lavender, the Art Department made the decision to replace them all with bougainvillea in a deeper fuchsia colour. The colour filmed beautifully on camera! There was absolutely no explanation for this—sometimes you just have to find the answer through trial and error.

Construction

The **Construction Coordinator** is in charge of the carpenters, painters, and labourers. **Never underestimate this team!** The construction team can be your **most valuable asset** in a crisis and save the shooting company hundreds of dollars or more with their expertise and practical solutions. They can efficiently resolve a Director's last-minute request while the entire shooting company stands by.

Construction spends your money! You have to have a great cooperation with the Construction Coordinator; they are like an additional Art Director.

They must try to stay on budget and let you know immediately if they are going to go over … they also find ways to do things less expensively.

Paint

As painter Clyde Zimmerman says, 'Color can be your best friend or your worst enemy'.

Your painters are as close to importance to your successful sets as your Set Decorator; some would say more so! When you look at a finished set, the first thing you see is the paint … and decoration. It *has to* be right!

It's not always about colour, either.

Many Cinematographers have paint 'agendas'; likes and dislikes, textures and finishes, flat or glossy—because *the paint on the walls is the canvas they use for their lights!*

Always do the Cinematographer the courtesy of asking what his preferences are for paint/finishes/textures … you will be surprised at how important this issue becomes as you gain experience.

Henry Bumstead used to say that the **painter is the most important tool in your toolbox!**

One stand-by painter on a Spielberg set of *Amazing Stories* saved the day in five minutes; the close-up of an actress looking out the window of the train on stage was stopped, because of some missing rivets around the train's window …

Thinking quickly, the painter grabbed a few lifesavers and some glue, glued the lifesavers to cover the missing rivet holes, and then painted them perfectly to blend in with the aged look of the antique steam engine!

A good painter can save almost anything; it's not always about colour. They are also responsible for making plywood appear to be marble, or painting fiberglass rocks to look

Figure 9.21 *The Kingdom*, bullet holes, paint and texture effects (styrofoam skin as plaster)

Figure 9.22 *Life of Pi*

natural and real, or aging 'new' kitchen cabinets to look thirty years old and used … a good painter is a gift, *'one of the best tools in your toolbox!'*

SPFX, Stunts, and Props

Your construction team may also be asked to build specifics for SPFX, STUNTS, and/or PROPS—as well as coming up with clever ways to hide things, such as cables, wires, mechanics, etc.

Always collaborate and lead your team with solid design solutions; every detail is important!

Figure 9.23 *The Ring*, shelter and dock built on location, aged and weathered to blend in with surroundings

Figure 9.24 *The Ring*, cabin, total build on location, aged and weathered to blend in with surroundings (note the moss on the roof)

Construction on Location

Construction on location presents its own set of issues; the Production Designer's job encompasses not only finding locations that will work for the project, but also selecting locations that are safe and relatively practical (for example, remote areas such as deserts and tropical jungles will not be easily accessible and may need custom roads built for the crew; water and power must also be considered).

An experienced Construction Coordinator with locations experience will be familiar with these conditions and will facilitate building of your sets economically.

The following examples of sets built on locations show just a sampling of the challenges presented to the Production Designer, the Art Department, and the Construction team:

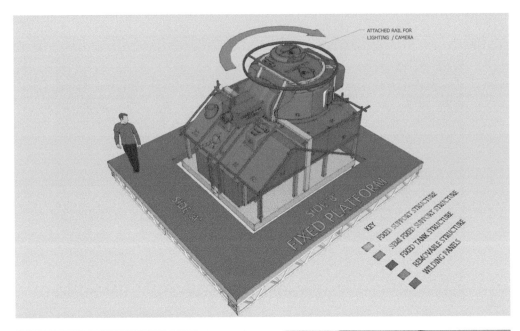

Figure 9.25 Fury, fibreglass phase, tank, drawing of tank set piece, colour keyed and tank in the paint shop

Figure 9.26 Fury, tank, walls wilded

Figure 9.27 *Maze Runner*, 4' foam gears (to look real)

Figure 9.28 Gravity,
space set on stage

Figure 9.29 *Book Thief*,
cobbles

Figure 9.30 *The Kingdom*, village set build actual build, from renderings

Figure 9.31 *The Kingdom*, village set build

Figure 9.32 *The Kingdom*, village set build in progress, from model

Figure 9.33 *The Kingdom*, village set details, see renderings

Figure 9.34 *The Kingdom,* set wrapped in styrofoam

Figure 9.35 *The Kingdom,* aerial view of construction on location

Figure 9.36 *The Kingdom*, blast effect debris

Figure 9.37 *The Kingdom*, finished rooftop set

Figure 9.38 *The Kingdom*, finished rooftop set, another view

Figure 9.39 *Lone Survivor,* camp set on location (Arizona dressed to look like Afghanistan)

CHAPTER 10

Studio Facilities

To me, the most interesting thing about Production Design is that every picture has its own problems.

—Bob Boyle (*North by Northwest, Cape Fear, Thomas Crown Affair, The Birds*)

Production Designer Dick Sylbert once said, 'I never film on back lots, because I don't believe in using "icons"'.

He preferred to <u>personally</u> find and scout locations for his pictures because he believed it was the job of the Production Designer to select and create the film's environment; this was part of the art of designing the visuals.

He learned this premise from working with Wm. Cameron Menzies, the talented architect, artist, and designer famous for his work on *Gone with the Wind*. Menzies was the first to receive the title of Production Designer. It was created for him by David O. Selznik, because the credit (or job description) of Art Director didn't seem to cover the complete involvement in the picture that Menzies provided; he even filmed some of the scenes himself, after carefully storyboarding (burning of the backlot/Atlanta).

Studio Facilities, Backlots, Warehouses, and Resources

This chapter will describe basic studio backlot filming procedures and operations. We will discuss considerations for filming in warehouses and learn about industry-standard terms, such as **stock units, scene docks, fire lanes,** and **permanent stage plans**.

Set-Building Locations

The production company will need to set up their offices somewhere and arrange for a place to build the sets for the show. In television, depending on the number of episodes ordered (the minimum is 6, but can be 9 or up to 13 at a time), these decisions are made for convenience and economy. A longer season of episodes requires more money and time.

It is the Production Designer's job to make the production company aware of any size requirements (height, width, double-wide doors, etc.) as early as possible, so that the appropriately sized stages and/or warehouses are selected.

Although economical on paper, it is never ideal for the production offices and sets to share the same space. In reality, construction is very noisy and dirty, and paint fumes can affect even the most good-natured Producers. It is best to have your own separate space for building sets and for the Construction Department.

When space is limited, sometimes construction has to work 'on a light'. This means that they are working so closely to the shooting company that the noise from the tools interferes with filming, so a red light is installed, and the construction crew is supposed to stop and wait for the light to go out.

It's not very efficient and really slows down the building of the sets. Construction should never share a stage with the shooting company.

Figure 10.1 Early furniture/prop storage on studio lot

A warehouse may or may not come with heating, cooling, phone, fax, Internet, or even restroom facilities. Be certain that the power is on and that everything is in working order. Remember, this will be home for you, the crew, and the shooting company for the next few months. Also, check the mobile phone service both inside and outside of the area.

Studio Stages and Facilities

Studio Stages

Stages on studio backlots are ideal because they were designed for filming. Sometimes they come equipped with **green beds** (which are overhead wooden catwalk grids from which to hang lights, and they are moveable), and they have extra-high, extra-wide barn doors that slide open to allow cranes, heavy equipment, staircases, furnishings, and lighting to load in easily.

Studio stages are also great because they usually have wooden floors to which sets can be nailed (instead of having to lay down a plywood floor over concrete, which is costly at both ends to put in, and then repair the floor later).

Wood floors also allow excavating for stairs, running water pipes, electrical cables, and even set crew members under the floors!

Each stage has a number and has been accurately measured by a professional draftsman. The resulting blueprint is called a **permanent stage plan**. This permanent stage plan is a floor plan, to scale, of the stage when it is completely empty. It will include any and all **permanent elements** of that particular stage.

A partial list of permanent elements might include the following:

- All doors, windows, and openings
- The location of any stairs or staircases
- A 'pit', or lower level under the stage, which is covered and might be opened up for use
- Any columns or beams

- Sometimes, overhead 'green beds' for lighting (these are moveable, and so are not always included on permanent stage plans)
- Plumbing/water sources, such as sinks and/or hose bibs
- Electrical boxes.

Stages also come with clearly marked **fire lanes**, **4' around the perimeter**, *which are to be kept clear at all times* for safety reasons.

Safety meetings are held regularly on studio lots, and union members are required to attend. Liability is a serious issue, and safety is a measure that every professional needs to be aware of at all times. Operating heavy equipment around dangerous electrical wiring is just one example of a safety concern, along with the usual saws, nail guns, paint fumes, and chemicals present on most set construction sites.

When a stage is rented from a studio, it may come equipped with many bonuses. These include access to the studio lot and its facilities. Since the loss of the old studio system, few studios keep full departments for Greens, hardware, Props, scenic backings, and stock units any more, but they can be found as outside vendors.

Some of these studio bonus facilities might be:

- A Commissary for meals
- A gift store
- A transportation department
- A department for **grip and electric**
- **Stock units**—set pieces, such as bay windows, staircases, and fireplace units, which are salvaged from previous shows
- **Props and furniture** rental
- **Special effects department** (where bullet **squibs** and minor explosions are designed)
- A plaster department (**staff shop**)
- A print shop for signs and graphics
- A **plumbing department** (with every size and style of bathtubs, sinks, and showers— even hot water heaters)
- A **hardware department**
- A **Greens Department**, or plant nursery.

The time saved by having these facilities in close proximity is priceless. Time is money in the film business, and in this case, an investment in a fully equipped studio stage rental makes everyone's job easier, especially that of the Production Designer!

The reason for this is that instead of having to shop for hardware for a large kitchen set or a backlot street, you can simply walk into the hardware department and rent it from them. They will even install it and strike it for a small fee, which saves you on labour (while also protecting their inventory from **loss and damage**, otherwise known as 'L&D'). It may even save you unnecessary purchases.

The early studio hardware departments were good for having great, unusual, antique and hard-to-find hardware.

The same goes for plumbing fixtures. Often, a bathtub or sink in a shot doesn't need to be functional, so it isn't necessary to purchase one; you can rent what you need from the plumbing department on the lot. They will also remove the rental at the end of shooting, saving you strike time and costly storage.

Scene Dock and Stock Units

Scene Dock

Sets are often designed, built, painted, dressed, filmed, and struck within a matter of days. For this reason, you should take advantage of everything a studio has to offer.

Not many studio scene docks are left anymore, but TV shows often keep a small 'scene dock' of cleated together, previously used walls, doors and windows and such that could be used in upcoming episodes to save money.

Stock Units

Stock units are fragments and parts of sets that have previously been used in other productions. These fragments are usually complicated parts of sets that are worth saving and reusing, such as:

- Staircases
- Gingerbread fretwork
- Archways
- The aisles of:
  - Doors
  - Window units
  - Window seats
  - Kitchens
  - Bars and back bars
  - Staircases
  - Fireplaces
  - Etc.

These stock units are useful because they don't have to be constructed from scratch—they have already been built. Stock units are located in the **scene dock**, which is a huge interior storage space on the studio lot. If the stock unit fits in with your set design, you can **rent it** and have it delivered to the stage or construction facility.

Once on stage, the construction team will assemble the sets using the stock units and new construction. Any necessary adjustments will be made to the units at this time. Then the team will paint plaster or wallpaper the walls to the design specifications.

This process saves time, money, and materials. It is a form of recycling. Of course, every Production Designer will make the units their own by modifying them in some way so that they are no longer recognizable. No one wants their sets to look familiar, or to appear 'copied' or unoriginal!

Figure 10.2 Studio
backlots, set pieces

The **scene dock** is where you will learn to tell an Eastlake door from a ladder door, a transom window from a 6-light mullioned window, and a Gothic archway from a Roman archway. Back bars, bay windows, cathedral doors, and stained-glass windows are found here. These units can be lifesavers when you need a quick set with a lot of character.

When you find units that you think you can use, you will have to reserve them and have your Set Designer measure and incorporate the units into your set plans (technical drawings). You will also need to describe the stock units to your Construction Coordinator so that they can plan ahead to make space for these set pieces before they are delivered.

Often, these units have issues that will need special attention. For example, since a unit has already been used, stored, and shuttled around, some set walls may be warped, and some plaster may be chipped and/or cracked. Window frames and doorjambs might not be in square (properly aligned). These are conditions your construction team will need to know about in advance, since they will be building some of your set using new materials and incorporating the stock units into the completed set. It is their job to make it all look seamless.

Studio Backlots (Part 1)

Continuity is the most important, because *it gets down to the shot*. Because it's just a series of shots that make a film, without it, we don't have anything. *Just building a set isn't enough; it's the shot that counts*.

Dream a little, even about opening titles and how they flow into the first scene. Everything has a continuity. It all makes sense.

The development of the picture is important, so I think you should start at the beginning.

—John DeCuir, Sr (*Cleopatra, Hello Dolly, The King and I*)

Studio backlots contain entire city streets and sometimes even neighbourhoods. As realistic as they appear, these are only facades. They may include a New York Street (a typical example of New York architecture), a generic version of 'Small Town USA', a European street, or even a pond or lake.

These additional filming options may work for scenes in your show and will save both time and money because you won't have to move away from the studio. Taking advantage of all that a studio has to offer is an efficient way to control the schedule.

Because the buildings are only facades, none of them have walls or are finished inside. They are meant to be filmed as **exteriors only**. (Interiors are filmed on stage sets or on location.) This presents challenges to the Production Designer, because even though there are no interiors, the windows must have window treatments and the doors must be accompanied by hardware, house numbers, appropriate mailboxes, trash cans, etc., in order to make the places look 'lived in', 'real', or authentic.

Occasionally, interiors are built within the sets on the backlot. The advantages are the ability to shoot continuous action from exterior to interior without cuts and the ability to have live action of people and vehicles as background action through the windows or storefronts behind the interior scenes. Great examples of this are the drugstore and the cafe interiors in *The Sting* and the doctor's office in *The Shootist*.

Before shooting can begin, even on these backlot streets, permission from the studio is required to paint graffiti in alleyways, hang neon signs above storefronts, and even to park picture vehicles in front of buildings. This permission is really a 'notification' to the studio of what you plan to do in any way to alter the look of their backlot. This is required because they have to be brought back to their original conditions (unless the studio approves leaving the changes).

A studio backlot is like a great big location. The main difference is that it has one corporate owner (the studio) and many departments, which saves you time and money.

These departments include:

- Transportation
- Hardware
- Plumbing
- Grip and electrical (grips deal with mechanical set moves; gaffers deal with anything electrical)
- Wardrobe
- Mill
- Sign shop
- Greens
- Props
- Drapery
- Accounting
- Special effects
- Paint
- Sculpture/plaster/staff shop
- Glass.

Some studios even have a bank on the lot for your convenience.

Using 'on-the-lot' services comes with the added bonus of familiarity; the **Greens Department**, for example, knows just where to put your selected shrubs and bushes because it has 'dressed' that street many times before. They will also help you choose the appropriate size and scale of items. And of course, since they are already on the lot, they can deliver, install, and strike your plants (for a fee) much more efficiently than an offsite vendor could.

The Warner Brothers ranch is an example of a location/studio facility complete with a lake and open fields. It is offsite from the Warner Brothers Studios lot. Once you have filmed there, it becomes easily recognizable to you in commercials and other projects because of the mature trees and placement of the lake and bridge. It offers the perfect picturesque setting and is already designed for shooting companies, with nearby crew parking.

Studio backlots need a lot of work just to make them 'look right'. However, when faced with the costs of travelling to a location in the country or building an entire Western street of facades, the time saved by filming on a backlot is often worth it, especially in television.

Be sure to do a thorough job of researching to find out what details make your city streetscape *unique*.

Figure 10.3 Warner Bros studio facilities

For example, colourful sidewalk flower stands tell us that we are in San Francisco; subway entrances, yellow cabs, and bishop's crook lampposts tell us we are in New York City.

Make sure that your street name signs, traffic signs, and car license plates are appropriate and accurate copies of the signs in your city. The more detail you can feed to the audience's subconscious perception, the more real your sets will be. Do everything you can to help sell the story.

When you are shooting a film or television show on a studio lot, you should familiarize yourself with all the studio has to offer. Visit each department as a courtesy, to introduce yourself—personal connections go a long way when you need that last-minute prop for a Director. It also helps if the other departments know who you are and what you're working on.

Warehouses

When presented with the option of building sets in a warehouse, you should always consider the following:

• Access for the crew and equipment
• Adequate parking (covered whenever possible, and safe—otherwise, plan to hire a security guard)
• Mobile phone service
• NOISE (do airplanes fly overhead, can you hear traffic through the building's walls, vibration through the floors from nearby trains or heavy equipment, and transformer or ballast hum from the existing lighting can pose problems that make recording dialogue very difficult).

In addition to the most basic facilities, which we take for granted (but which are not always provided, such as restrooms, power, heating, and cooling), you should also think about the **weather** and how it might affect the building(s) you will be using.

As an example, imagine you have agreed to work in a warehouse with a corrugated tin roof. During a rainstorm, the noise will becomes so deafening that filming is impossible. In the heat of the day, the tin will become so hot that the warehouse feels like an oven. After the sun goes down, if there is no insulation, the temperature can be frigid. AC (air conditioning) and heating units can always be brought in, but they are noisy, clumsy, and not very effective.

Be aware of the conditions in any space *before* you agree to use it for construction or filming needs. **All physical conditions are your responsibility**, so try to anticipate any problems in advance. It may prove very expensive in the long run to build sets and film in a 'discounted' warehouse.

Any space used for the production should offer the most basic facilities in working order and meet required health standards. Rodents, roaches, and other pest infestations may not show up on the day you are scouting, so ask the hard questions and get confirmation, in writing, that the required standards are met, especially if you are uncertain about a location in any way.

Cause for uncertainty might include high-crime neighbourhoods (theft can be an issue), proximity to chemical plants (air may be unsafe to breathe), and deserted or abandoned areas that may present vermin infestations or other health and safety hazards. It may be tempting to think that these considerations are someone else's job, but never assume or take for granted that they have been addressed!

A good Production Designer is **always aware** of the **physical environment**, both on and off camera. Safety of the cast and crew is paramount at all times; this awareness will serve you well. Once you sign off on something, you become liable (responsible) for it.

Taking some additional caution regarding the safety and comfort of the cast and crew will more than pay for any additional costs upfront. A happy crew works faster, harder, and has nothing to complain about. The positive morale on set will create an atmosphere that allows everyone to do their best work.

Always be aware of the working conditions you are agreeing to, and make it your priority to secure the very best the budget will allow. The long-term results of this simple decision will reward you and the entire shooting company many times over.

Studio Backlots (Part 2)

When I started my first job at Universal Studios, just being on a major studio lot was a very big deal.

It was just like I imagined; I saw actors in wild costumes, set pieces on slow-moving flat-beds heading for the stages, movie stars being driven to the sets in golf carts, carpenters and painters riding bicycles from stage to stage, groups of executives in suits and sunglasses, and wardrobe trailers and prop trucks parked outside of stages where shooting was going on.

I passed Stage 28, famous for the *Phantom of the Opera* film, and the Alfred Hitchcock bungalow (where he worked until retirement) on my way to the Commissary for lunch.

The magic of the backlot was everywhere: Jaws Lake, the Psycho House, Back to the Future Square, New York Street, Western Town, Mexican Village, European Street, and the neighbourhood for the Academy Award winning film *To Kill a Mockingbird* (built by Production Designer Henry Bumstead, when he rescued several old houses from the wrecking ball and moved them to the backlot, thereby creating the realism and the authenticity that movie is known for).

The Munster House, Wisteria Lane, and *Leave It to Beaver* were all part of backlot history, as well.

Warner Brothers backlot has *The Waltons* and Mayberry from *The Andy Griffith Show*.

What was hard to understand for me at that time, was how empty the buildings were; many of them are fronts only, facades, with no sides or rear walls, and no interiors. When you walk around these facades, you will see stage braces, propping them up and many of them were open to the sky … meaning no roofs!

They looked like abandoned buildings from the back. Looking closely, I noticed there were no mailboxes or house numbers, or even street signs. This is to allow each show to customize and tailor the buildings and streets to suit their individual projects.

- Alleys are swept clean and empty; each show dresses them with trash cans, pallets, graffiti, etc.
- Windows have no window treatments
- Sidewalks have no litter, cigarette butts, or gum
- No trees, flowers, or window boxes come with backlot streets or neighbourhoods.

In other words, no 'personal touches' or evidence of individuality are evident anywhere; this is to keep them a 'blank slate' for the next project to use.

If a hit show films a particular brick wall with custom graffiti, it must be restored to the original condition. A new show or project may want to use the same brick wall for a different project in a completely different time period, or part of the country, for one reason, and for another—well, no one wants to be called out for reusing a set from a previous show or Designer.

The unspoken rules of the trade are to always alter and make it your own … this is a creative field, after all.

After a while, even with changes and alterations, backlots can become easily recognizable simply because their layouts are familiar; the relationships of buildings to one another, architectural details such as columns, doors and windows, even rooflines give them away.

Once you become familiar with the backlots of the various studios, it's easy to spot them for what they are. This is because Production Designers have the most intimate relationship with the architecture on a film than any other department.

PD Dick Sylbert once said that he 'never used backlots for any films because he didn't believe in using icons', or artificial, 'generic', 'paint by numbers' sets.

Instead, he preferred to scout and find all of the locations for his movies himself. He treated them as characters, in and of themselves.

The house in *Baby Doll*, the campus for *Carnal Knowledge*, and the neighbourhoods for *Who's Afraid of Virginia Woolf* and *Chinatown*, to name a few.

He did, however, agree to film on a backlot once—for the film *Dick Tracy*, which was a comic book and 'all about icons'.

Still, backlots serve a unique purpose for television shows, commercials, and music videos, especially when time is short and the schedule involves night filming.

Figure 10.4 *Life of Pi*, backlot, blue screen (before)

Figure 10.5 *Life of Pi*, computer generated image of backlot street (after)

Figure 10.6 Burbank
Studios backlot

Figure 10.7 Universal
Studios backlot

For controlled do-overs (re-shoots) like on *Blade Runner* or *Dick Tracy*, *Batman*, or a Western town, where the entire environment is created and controlled, backlots can work very well for those.

Backlots offer control, security, and 24/7 access ... and are often convenient, due to being close to Production Offices and facilities on the lot.

When you will be using any backlot for filming, challenge yourself as a Designer to 'make it real', make it different, make it unique in some way ... this will make you a better Designer and you will earn respect from your peers who may recognize the lot, but will appreciate your creativity.

CHAPTER 11

Backings

I rode in the Bosun Chair, or open-air bucket, and took a camera down the face of Mount Rushmore to get the shots we needed to create those realistic backings for North by Northwest. The still photographer didn't want to do it, so I did it myself.

Back at the studio, for the shots of them looking down, we stretched a backing across the stage floor, from the pictures I took that day looking down from that chair.

The film turned out pretty good; we couldn't have done those scenes without backings'.

—Bob Boyle (*North by Northwest, The Birds, Gaily, Gaily*)

There is a great documentary film, *The Man On Lincoln's Nose*, about Production Designer Bob Boyle and his experience designing the film, *North by Northwest* for Alfred Hitchcock.

North by Northwest required several backings of Mount Rushmore to be custom-made, for the critical action shots to be filmed on the Rushmore set built on stage.

Hitchcock was famous for his desire for control, which is why he preferred filming on stages rather than locations. He planned his shots meticulously, to the point where it was often said 'you could film his storyboards and see the whole movie, shot by shot'.

To accurately reproduce the backings needed, Bob Boyle and a professional still photographer flew to the National Monument to take a series of photos which would match the shots and camera angles Hitch had prepared.

When they arrived at the top of the mountain, the still photographer panicked and refused to do the job.

Being a practical man, Bob stepped in to the harness of the bosun's chair, carrying the heavy still camera, and was lowered down the face of Mount Rushmore to shoot the stills himself. He knew all of Hitchcock's desired shots and camera angles because they had discussed and designed them together, and he was familiar with the storyboards.

One of the most successful stills he took was the POV (point of view) looking straight down, into the rock canyon; this huge finished backing was stretched across the stage floor (not hung from the ceiling, per usual), and created the illusion of height and perspective along the (artificial) rock set, which was built to duplicate part of Mt. Rushmore on the stage.

On screen for only a matter of seconds, the shot is believable and the illusion is complete.

Figure 11.1 *North by Northwest* backing, Rushmore, Production Designer Bob Boyle

Figure 11.2 *North by Northwest* backing, Rushmore with actors Cary Grant and Eva Marie Saint

In this chapter we will define backings and discuss the various types used in film and television production. We will also cover placement of backings and considerations in making them as effective as possible. This chapter will touch on the use of scale models, miniatures, and special effects. Finally, we will discuss the Greens Department and some ways a Production Designer can work effectively with them.

The Best Book Written About One of Our Crafts … Ever.

Richard M. Isackes and Karen L. Maness. *The Art of the Hollywood Backdrop*. New York: Regan Arts, 2014.

I have a lot of books about motion picture design. I don't pass them up when I find them in used bookstores, or online … or anywhere else, for that matter. Karen Maness and Richard Isackes have produced the finest book in my collection, the one that now lives on the coffee table and that I show to anyone who visits my home. It is filled cover to cover with breathtaking images of painted backings, archival behind-the-scenes photographs, and original photos often taken by the artists themselves to record their work. Ms. Maness was helped in her quest to compile this material by the ADG's archivist, Rosemarie Knopka, and the collected material that she is preserving for the Guild. This book also includes oral histories from the surviving artists or their family members, irreplaceable stories of this extraordinary craft. It is a mix of film history, art criticism, technical solutions, and beautiful film settings. It is, simply, the first book that every working designer needs to own.

—by Michael Baugh, editor and book collector

Figure 11.3 Backings at JC Backings scenic studio

Backings

You will not be able to film on location for every set or show. There is more to building a good set on stage than just layout, architecture, and mouldings.

A backing is a specially created background image. Backings are hung, erected, or projected outside a set—behind windows, doors, balconies, rooftops, etc.—that completes the set's exterior view. You will need to decide exactly what will be seen outside the windows of the set. Your breakdown sheets will tell you whether it is day, night, or both. This affects the type of backing you choose as well as the lighting.

This is when your ability to imagine and visualize comes in handy. Where, in the script, are we? What city? Which country? What type of neighbourhood? What part of the country? Are you on the East Coast, in the South, in the Western states, or in the North? Is this an affluent/upscale area, or a downscale area?

Does the neighbourhood have trees, and if so, what kind? If it is a high-rise office building, **how high is it**? Are they on the second floor, or the fifty-second floor? What should be seen outside the windows—other buildings? A river? A beach? A construction site?

Figure 11.4 *Hail, Caesar!* sky backing

Figure 11.5 *Hail, Caesar!* sky backing (with set pieces)

Figure 11.6 *Towering Inferno*, painted backing

Figure 11.7 Painted backings in Sky-Lit Studio/ Warner Brothers Studios

Figure 11.8 *History of the World*, painted backing

Figure 11.9 *On A Clear Day*, painted backing

Figure 11.10 Painted backing, detail

Figure 11.11 Painted backing: scenic. From left: Ferrell, Jimmy Finger, Bob Oberbeck, Unknown, and Gordon Butcher

Figure 11.12 Painted backing, scenic. *Bierstadt*

Backing Types

There are many backings available to rent. These are grouped in albums and numbered for ease of ordering. Television doesn't always have the time to create new, original backings, though some films do have these resources. You will become familiar with the books and albums of backings fairly quickly. In time, you will even recognize a backing you have used when it pops up in a commercial or another project.

When selecting a backing, you first must decide what **type** of backing you will need. Do you need it for day, night, or both? Will it be a painted backing (painted by hand) or a translight (translite—an old term from the days when tinted sheets of black and white translucent photographic materials were used). The word 'translate' has become a generic term for photo backings today, with the actual material called 'Chromatrans' and/or 'Duratrans'. Both are a colour photographic material which can be backlit through the transparent backing material.

Always talk to your Cinematographer and include them in this decision. It is their responsibility to light the backing properly, and they will usually have a preference.

The backings are separated into categories in the books, to make it easy for you to find the type you are looking for, and they are also listed by **size**. You must know the size of your stage and the sizes of the window opening(s) and doors that you will need the backing to serve. Always add a few feet on either side, in case a Director decides to use an angle needing a little more coverage than required.

Once selected, you need to be sure the backing is available. Because other companies are renting backings too, it is always a good idea to **know your dates required for shooting!** If the backing is needed for a permanent set, it will be priced for rental for the run of the show, usually at a discount based on the number of days. Otherwise, it will be considered a 'short-term' rental, which is for one week or less.

If your selection is not available on your dates, you need to select a plan B. It is always a good idea to have a second backing selected in advance, because occasionally things just happen and your first choice, though promised, may not be available when you need it. Being prepared ensures efficiency and peace of mind.

Backings are delivered to the stage and are hung with an experienced team that is familiar with the ins and outs of handling backings of all types. You will be asked to be there on stage to spot the backing. This important step in the process is when you place the backing in the precise location you desire.

You will want certain things to be seen outside the windows of your set and placed in an exact position in relation to your backing. If you want a branch of the tree outside the kitchen window, for example, you must be there to say so! The backing will then be adjusted accordingly.

The trick to making a backing appear more 'real' than simply a fake back drop, is *movement*.

The camera doesn't like to linger too long on a static backdrop, because without any movement, the audience realizes something is 'off' … life is not *still*.

The illusion of movement can be suggested through use of back projection, through lighting, atmosphere (smoke, rain, snow, etc.) or through the use of actual objects moving in front of a backing. This would include wind through tree branches, a car or vehicle pulling up to divert attention, even animals or moving set pieces, like a waterwheel.

Many backings don't look real because they are in too sharp focus; there is no atmospheric perspective (softening the image due to atmosphere and distance).

Softening the backing can be achieved with bobinette or by asking the backing company to print the backing slightly out of focus.

One Art Director had the challenge of making a night scene using an ocean backing appear 'real' for a romantic scene in the moonlight.

The lighting was perfect, yet the backing still lacked something; it looked 'flat'.

Suddenly, he had an idea. After speaking to the Prop Master, he returned with several strings of tiny white Christmas lights that blinked. He taped them to the BACK side of the backing.

He then artfully cut small holes throughout the backing in a pattern to simulate sparkling moonlight, and blacked-out a few of the lights (so they wouldn't be so regularly spaced).

The end result was magical; it was as if the ocean waves were moving in the distance, and the moonlight twinkled on the surface … perfect for the scene! In theatres, no one could tell it was a stage set with a backing and not the Pacific Ocean in the distance.

The same effect can be achieved on a daylight backing by taping crinkled cellophane strips at random to the face of the 'water' and gently agitating them with an off-camera ritter fan, causing the 'water' to glitter with reflections of the backing lighting on the moving cellophane tapes.

Be sure to allow plenty of **throw**—which means the distance between the back of the set wall and the backing itself. Too close never works and results in a blurry view. Too far away risks distortion. This placement decision should include input from your Cinematographer because their crew will be lighting the backing. All of this takes time, so make sure your backing(s) are scheduled well in advance of shooting.

Figure 11.13 *Hail, Caesar!* backing, water tank

Also remember that backings will take up valuable space on your stage, outside of your set doors and windows. Be sure to factor in this additional floor space for stage braces and/or overhead rigging when you are spotting your sets on permanent stage plans. Listing every detail you can on your floor plans is professional and will ensure clear communication between departments.

Remember that as you get closer to filming, your set will be filled with the crews from several different departments at once. Try to give each of them notice ahead of time so that there isn't an army of ladders overlapping for lighting, set decorating, painting, and construction because everyone is trying to do their jobs at the same time.

In television, unfortunately, the time frame is always very tight. Professional crews learn to overlap and to work together when they have to, even when conditions are not ideal. It is considerate and respectful to try to schedule and organize every department well in advance whenever possible.

Figure 11.14 *Hail, Caesar!* backing, submarine

Matte Painting

Matte paintings are used to '*matte something out of the frame*', or to replace with something else.

This was a skill used before the days of green-and-blue screen. Matte paintings were used to **create or** to **substitute backdrops in combination with the exposed film footage**.

Some mattes were painted on glass, fixed in perspective in front of the camera, lit carefully, and used in actual shots of the film.

This was a talent learned, and rarely in use today. There was an Art Director who was so good at painting glass mattes, he would do them on site, hours before the shot was needed.

They would be camera-ready backgrounds exactly in scale and matching the colour palette, usually outdoors.

Directors found this useful for many reasons; sometimes it was easier to paint out a distraction than to shoot around it!

Since the computer has taken over visual effects in movies and TV, matte paintings are extremely rare these days, as CG has pretty much taken over all of those types of visual tricks (glass mattes, foreground miniatures, and foreground metal mattes).

Figure 11.15 *Life of Pi*, blue screen, water tank and boats

Figure 11.16 *Lone Survivor*, blue screen (with registration marks for effects)

Figure 11.17 *Patriots Day*, green screen city shot (before and after)

Models

Making scale models of sets takes time. A scale model is a physical replica of your set. This is a usually a luxury mainly reserved for films, unless it is a permanent set on a television show.

You may have time to have your Set Designer construct a **foam core model** of a permanent set. This is done by simply gluing down the set floor plan and four elevations (walls) onto a large sheet of 1/4" white foam core material. These plans and elevations are cut very cleanly so that they fit into the corners neatly when glued together using white glue. The model is then mounted to an appropriate base, such as a 1.2" foam core, balsa wood, or plywood, and any extras (small shrubs, cars, trees, etc.) are added for realism. A model is **always** in perfect scale (1/4", standard) to the build.

Note: It's wise to cut out your window openings **before** the elevations (walls), windows, and door openings are glued in place!

This model is an excellent tool for the entire production team. The **Director** can see the spaces for blocking and planning scenes, the **Cinematographer** can create interesting lighting opportunities, and the **Set Decorator** can see the number and sizes of walls and can make plans for paintings, artwork, wall sconces, and shelves. The model also shows the number and sizes of windows—useful information when planning for curtains, blinds, and window treatments. Some Art Directors/Production Designers may even draw or place scale model furniture in order to help sell the concept and communicate the design to all departments.

Models are another mark of a true professional. Many questions concerning the action and filming of the script can easily be resolved by referring to the set model. It enables everyone to visualize the set before it is built. Any problems or red flags can be addressed at this time. This saves money because supplies have not yet been purchased and labour has not yet been expended. It is a good idea to develop the habit of using models whenever possible. They will more than pay for themselves.

Figure 11.18 *Life of Pi*, model with Amber figure (before)

Figure 11.19 Model, blue screen, *Life of Pi* (after)

Miniatures

Miniatures are just what they sound like: miniature versions of a larger set or set piece. They are usually built around 20–30 per cent to scale. This proportion allows for enough detail on the miniature to suggest the full-size object on camera without distortion. A miniature is very much like a model airplane or car, only larger. When properly done, miniatures are in between full size and kit size. They are **always** to scale.

Movie miniatures may have moving parts, and present challenges to all departments. Lighting, atmosphere, and even actors have to consider the size the miniature is intended to be on screen in order to 'sell it' (make it believable) on film. Famously, *Titanic* used miniatures, as did the *The Wizard of Oz*.

Perspective is also a critical consideration when filming with miniatures. **Forced perspective** is a theatrical term, meaning that the natural perspective is **compressed** into a smaller or shorter distance using visual tricks. The result should accurately resemble the natural effect whenever possible. Occasionally, stage floors are **ramped up** (gently sloped upward at an angle toward the distance). Television rarely uses miniatures because they are costly and take a long time to build.

Figure 11.20 *Tora! Tora! Tora!* miniature

Figure 11.21 The Grand Budapest Hotel miniature (in front of green screen)

CHAPTER 12

Make-Up, Speciality Character Design, and Creatures

Effects are our paintbrushes!

—Jim Bissell (*ET, Mission Impossible—Rogue Nation, Monuments Men, Good Night, and Good Luck*)

It is crucial that you be kept in the loop regarding any and all Special Effects designs, because YOU are responsible for the look of the entire film!

Production Designers *unify the vision and bring the vision to reality*.

The Production Designer should try to oversee the creature Illustrators/Designers, even though it sounds like the responsibility of the 'Make-Up Department', or Wardrobe, and/ or Props.

Even if the design has somewhat been set, there are important nuances that can be controlled. *There is an art to all effects*, involving colour, texture, shape, and details important to the tone or vision.

Designing is still the same; the creative process hasn't changed.

The fundamentals of dramatic design must always be considered; ***execution of the vision is the Production Designer's responsibility***.

Be sure to be included in any and all design meetings, even at your own expense. You will be accepted as the leader of the design process when you participate and contribute.

The origins of what we do come from storytelling; creature and character designs require us to 'think like an actor', as Production Designer Jim Bissell says.

His acting background in theatre has helped him to create sets based on *characters*.

'We give experiences'. We think, 'what is the audience going to *feel?*'

We create a space for the actor that is visceral; it follows that we would also be involved in the creation of the actor's *character*.

—Jim Bissell (*ET, Mission Impossible—Rogue Nation, Monuments Men, Good Night, and Good Luck*)

Inspiration can come at any time, from any source …

'sometimes I'll <u>hear</u> a set before I see it' (Jim Bissell)—when it doesn't come, I take a walk or do a crossword.

We need to understand the film first; orientation dictates style.

—Jim Bissell (*ET, Mission Impossible—Rogue Nation, Monuments Men, Good Night, and Good Luck*)

Story and character always come FIRST; design must be appropriate to both the story and the character.

Passion is ESSENTIAL! We conjure up images in our imagination, then we sketch, make models, create visuals of all types to bring the imagination into reality.

Special character design is about light and shade and how the make-up captures light and creates shadows … these design principles are ESSENTIAL to good character design!

<u>Art is the foundation; shape, line, colour, texture, form, and rhythm</u> are fundamentals for creation.

This includes all effects and speciality design, which often involves make-up for aging a character (as in ***The Curious Case of Benjamin Button***, where the character ages

Figure 12.1 Joel Harlow, speciality make-up

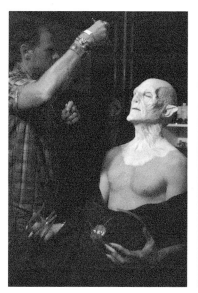
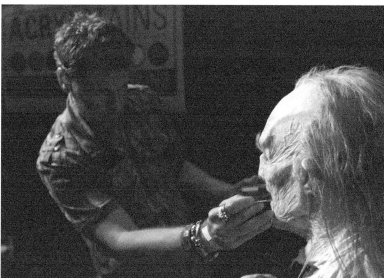

Figure 12.2 Joel Harlow, speciality make-up

Figure 12.3 Creature make-up, *The Walking Dead*

Figure 12.4 *The Thing*

backwards), full or partial facial masks, as in **The Mask**, **Batman**, **The Hobbit**, and facial disguises as in **Catch Me If You Can**, **Sherlock Holmes**, and **Jason Bourne**.

These looks can make or break a project, and although under the supervision of the Make-Up Department, become the responsibility of the Production Designer to ensure continuity and clarity of the Director's vision.

Although these looks have nothing to do with set design or locations, the way the characters appear involve DESIGN, and everything related to or involving design rests with you.

Creatures and comic book heroes involve design as well.

Sometimes, the design has been established, as in **Dick Tracy** or **Spiderman**, or even **The Hulk**.

Other times, the creatures must be original, unlike anything ever seen before ... and it's up to the Production Designer to suggest or outline the creation before any of the speciality make-up and effects departments become involved. Examples of these would be **Alien** and **ET**.

Figure 12.5 *Alien*

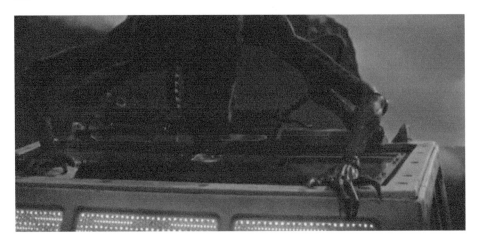

Figure 12.6 *ET*

Figure 12.7 *Avatar*

Figure 12.8 *Guardians of the Galaxy*

Your original ideas will probably evolve and/or change over the course of many meetings (apart from your other duties of building sets, prepping locations, designing signs and graphics, etc.); it is still important that you are PREPARED with your own concepts for the vision to be produced.

Never underestimate the power of a simple sketch, outlining an approach to the task at hand.

Technicians are not designers! Their skill lies in other areas.

Become accustomed to handling everything design-related for every project you are part of; this will <u>train those around you</u> to come to you with any and all design questions, for which you will have the answers.

It is extra work, and extra hours, but well worth the time and effort made. One lame creature or character onscreen can make a drama a comedy … for all the wrong reasons!

Computer-designed animation should be treated with the same care and respect; the entire production needs to acknowledge that all design rests first with the Production Designer; this ensures integrity of vision and continuity for the project.

Just because you are not an animator is no excuse for 'opting out' of those crucial meetings where character design is often discussed and formed … *<u>you are responsible for the look of the project, in its entirety</u>*.

Don't allow technical terms or phrases to supersede good design! If you are not familiar with a buzz-word or phrase, ask! Chances are, most people in the room are intimidated or unsure as well; technology changes rapidly, as does terminology.

You will show assertiveness and confidence by **calling for clarity**—and will be appreciated for it!

CHAPTER 13

Stunts, Visual FX, Special FX

Know when the effects company can add something and know when it's better to do it the old-fashioned way. Design it yourself for post … they can't always afford it in post.

Your job is to do as much as you possibly can—take a RUN at it! This way, you are helping everyone around you so each of you looks better! At the end of the day, your name is on it … it's *your responsibility*.'

—Jeannine Oppewal (*LA Confidential, Pleasantville, Catch Me If You Can, Seabiscuit*)

SPFX: Special Effects

Special effects is an area that has grown from basic candy glass and balsa wood breakaways to encompass the tech field of CGI, or computer-generated images. CGI has become so relatively inexpensive that it is common practice on TV shows now.

CGI is often the only way to create certain images on a show or film within the allowed budget and schedule.

Visual FX (VFX), Special FX (SPFX) and stunts are often interrelated; for example, a set extension may use green screen and a stunt, which involves rigging or special breakaway set pieces, or even VFX for environment.

The challenges to the Production Designer and the Art Department are multiplied, depending on the types of effects used. Motion capture, 3D, and VR (virtual reality) all could fill a separate, and unique, chapter.

Simple effects like rain, snow, wind, bullet hits, breaking glass, and balsa furniture, etc. are usually managed in-house, making supervision and control easy.

The same goes for explosions, fire, and pyrotechnics, which are effects only produced by certified experts.

VFX, backings (green and blue screen) and old-school techniques such as miniatures, matte paintings and optical printing might be separated from CGI. As long as you are familiar with the possibilities, you are able to offer practical options that are also well designed.

The main thing to remember is to **stay involved in every step of the effects process**, from initial discussions and design solutions to the final end result.

Figure 13.1 *ET*, set, smoke FX (1982)

Figure 13.2 *ET*, miniature on stage (1982)

Educate yourself on different types of effects and participate in all meetings and discussions—this will ensure continuity in the look of the project as well as *establish a collaboration between all departments*.

Computer and digital effects are costly, time-consuming, and are differentiated from practical effects executed on set. Effects on set are known as special effects, while CGI is referred to as visual effects. These effects involve entirely new subcontractors of the Art Department. The subcontractors work independently of you and your team. Often, they are hired at the end of a shoot, by which time you are off the project and on to something else. This can present problems with consistency and with the design approach.

Figure 13.3 *Unbroken*, outdoor tank with 24' high blue screen surround

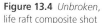

Figure 13.4 *Unbroken*, life raft composite shot

Figure 13.5 *Unbroken*, mock-up of B-24 on gimbal rig on stage

Because subcontractors work for an outside company, challenges to maintaining 'the look' are inevitable. An Art Director from the FX company may have ideas that differ from yours. Due to differing ideas and communication challenges, less-than-satisfactory FX are sometimes produced and the original Production Designer is re-hired for re-shoots. This issue is under discussion with the Art Directors Guild, as, clearly, it directly affects the look of a project, and, in a perfect world, continuity should reign.

Today, the best you can hope for is *a close working relationship with the outside team early on* and with everyone involved, including the Director. When you are the Production Designer, keeping yourself in the loop whenever possible ensures continuity in the look of the project.

Often, this means showing up on your own time (unpaid) to view what it is the CGI team is creating since the Production Designer is not officially part of this process. At this stage, the Production Designer may or may not have input, and little or no control and/or influence. As independent contractors, CGI workers answer only to the Director and themselves once the deal has been approved by production. Whether paid or unpaid, the Production Designer's presence, input, and collaboration can be extremely beneficial throughout this effects process. Try to collaborate whenever possible.

Green and blue screens are VFX that can be considered backings or even sets, depending on the extent of their use. In general, green screen usually indicates indoor filming (such as a weather map), and blue screen is used for outdoor, or exterior, filming.

These are not hard and fast rules. Sometimes, a VFX company will use blue screen INDOORS on a stage set using mountain climbers, for example, to project an image of a beautiful Swiss mountain range in the distance.

Figure 13.6 *Hail, Caesar!* Green Screen, EXT studio lot, period, (BEFORE)

Figure 13.7 *Hail, Caesar!* Green Screen, EXT studio lot (AFTER)

Figure 13.9 *Gravity*, green screen set

Special Effects—Special Visual Effects (SPFX/VFX)

Traditionally, Special Effects meant using one or all of three techniques to expand on and blend into the action or performances captured by traditional Cinematography.

The first technique is called Physical Effects or Practical Effects or Mechanical Effects and in the old days just plain Special Effects. Special Effects Men (and rarely Women) were part of the regular crew. They provided rain rigging or snow rigging or snow on the set, water effects like waves in a tank, smoke or fog for atmosphere, fire in a fireplace or for an entire burning set, explosions, bullet hits, arrow or spear hits, breakaway glass, breakaway props or set pieces, special mechanical props, brighter head lights for cars in day for night scenes, cable rigs to pull vehicles into or out of a scene, rigs to flip vehicles, wire rigs to fly actors or stunt people or yank them out of the set or into the air or against a wall, and so on. A good example of Physical Effects is in a dry for wet scene (examples are under water submarine scenes like those in *The Hunt for Red October* or the opening or closing scenes of *The Shape of Water*. A set is built to look like the bottom of the ocean or a 'water filled room'. The Effects Team fills the set with smoke (atmosphere) and places very large shallow pans of water with broken shards of mirror in the bottom and agitates the water. The Gaffer directs light through the water, bounces it off the broken mirror, back through the agitated water and it is picked up throughout the smoke atmosphere as wavy light. The Cinematographer shoots at speed and (Special Effects) wire suspended actors and props seem to float in slow motion as if they were hindered by the density of water. Shooting through a large fish tank with minute air bubbles flowing up can add to the effect as well.

The second technique was the use of miniatures or hanging miniatures. Hogwarts was a miniature in the first *Harry Potter* movies, The B-29 and the P-40s in *Empire of the Sun* were large scale miniatures, large enough to use lawn mower engines for their propellers. They actually flew by remote control and the P-40 had a miniature pilot that turned his head and waved at Christian Bale. Many of the collapsing buildings in *Earthquake* were miniatures and all the trucks and cars that fell off the freeway and the freeway itself were miniatures. The dam that collapses was a 90-foot-wide miniature replica of the Mulholland Dam in the Hollywood Hills. The water released smashed miniature houses the size of desks. They were all built and rigged by the effects team to do what they did. The early *Star Wars* movies were full of miniature sets and miniature spacecraft made by Special Effects shops. They were shot with motion control cameras. Motion Control is a whole different subject to study but it is the beginning of computer effects, computer controlled cameras that provided film sequences that were composited in optical cameras. That technique culminated in Technical Academy Award winning optical cameras that could hold dozens of different film strips and moving matte negatives and optically blend up to 40 or 50 motion control passes. All the pieces were meticulously crafted and painted miniatures. The X-wing fighters and the Death Star 'canyons' they flew into were miniatures. There is a 30-foot-long, meticulously rendered miniature of the airship in many shots of *The Hindenburg*. That miniature hangs in the Smithsonian's Air and Space Museum in Washington D.C. A miniature aircraft flies down a miniature Hollywood Blvd in *1941*. The Aircraft is 'flown' along a wire rig that allows the aircraft to roll as it screams along the canyon between the tall buildings.

The third technique was called Optical Effects. One part of that has been described above. Optical Cameras are used to blend Matte Shots, Blue Screen Shots, other filmed elements and the live action shots together photographically. Optical Cameras are large, as long as a Volkswagen and one third of its width. Mounted on their beds are Cameras and Projectors and Film Reels that allow the sandwiching of positive and negative matte film elements and the projection of them directly into the lens of the photographing camera, creating a new piece of film with the combined images.

The Matte Shot is one of the most basic and original of the Optical Effects (now called Visual Effects). It is true film magic, called The Invisible Art because most of the time you don't realize it's there, it contributes to the story, it doesn't distract or call attention to itself. Black Mattes are cut and lined up in front of the lens of a pin registered camera. The matte cuts out of the photographed image the area we want to change to help tell the story. The area exposed below, above or next to the matte holds the action within the location or set. Next a painting is done to blend into the shot and it is photographed with the same lens and camera, the painting has the same lighting and perspective as the unmatted portion of the shot. The identical focus, depth of field and atmosphere in the unmatted part of the shot must be in the painting as well. In the first *Star Wars* movie there is a shot of our heroes approaching Han Solo's space ship in the huge landing bay of the Death Star. The actors, the painted floor, the entry ramp of the space ship, some busy extras and some props are real; everything else is painted except a miniature space craft that was shot with a motion control camera and optically matted in to look like it flies in and lands during the shot.

In the movie *Mame* there is a scene where our heroes enter a huge Ballroom in a Large Mansion. The lower walls were built on a stage at Warner Bros. Studio, the upper walls and ornate Domed Ceiling were a painting.

Since the beginning of motion picture making up until now there are matte shots in every other movie we see. Medieval Castles, Roman Temples, cities on distant planets, streets of Chicago and New York in the 1930s. There are 65 matte shots in *The Hindenburg* blending the painted 1,000-foot-long airship into 1930s German and American environments that don't exist anymore.

Another type of optical effect is blue screen or more common today, green screen and a few times in the past, yellow screen (using sodium vapor lighting to blend birds into the blue sky in Hitchcock's movie *The Birds*). It is another way to blend live action and minimal amounts of set pieces with backgrounds that don't really exist or are too costly to build. It is also a method of placing actors in a place that is too dangerous or too difficult to reach. Actors can interact with themselves (in a different role) with the use of Blue Screen. Blue Screen was often called Traveling Mattes in the past because of the distinct advantage it had over Matte Shots. A matte shot is anchored to its painting, the camera cannot move because the cutline and the perspective of painting cannot change if the camera pans or dollies. In a Blue Screen shot each frame of the shot can show a slightly different blue patch and it can be altered by an actor moving into it or props or set pieces cutting in to it. A negative black patch can be made of each frame that will adjust and vary the matte of each frame in perfect movement with the original shot. The matte 'travels' with the action and allows the background to fit into the shot perfectly no matter what the foreground action. Today's sophistication of this method using Green Screen is far more flexible and the camera can now move with great freedom. We will touch on that later.

These three categories of Special Effects have more variations and combinations, whole books are written about all the inventions that were extrapolated from these basic ideas. Many shots are made using the combinations of all three elements, for instance a physical explosion rigged by a Special Effects technician, shot against blue screen, and optically married to a miniature set or a matte shot is one of the staples of early *Star Wars* movies. In this case it wasn't Blue Screen actually, it was 'Black

Screen', the explosion was shot against a black backing. The variations on the basics are part of your learning experience, it's an open-ended, ever changing art.

When the Academy of Motion Pictures Arts and Sciences began giving Oscars for Special Effects work, three Oscars went to the department heads of each type of effect. *Earthquake* and *The Hindenburg* both received three statuettes for Special Effects. One for Physical Effects (fire, explosions, falling buildings, crashing airships, coordination with stunts, etc.); one for Miniatures and one for Optical Effects (Matte Shots and Blue Screen).

Another very common use of Blue Screen is to place the moving scenery behind planes, trains and automobiles. Blue screen has pretty much replaced Rear Projection and Front Projection. The same rules apply, camera angles need to be matched, lenses and lighting need to be matched. Images seen in reflecting glass, physical light or shadows passing over the actors or vehicle need to be applied, etc. If you haven't reached the level of digital compositing, the images still need to be resolved in the optical camera.

Another way to solve visual problems is with the use of 'In Camera Effects'. Hanging Miniature set pieces, Glass Shots or Foreground Cut Out Paintings are examples of this kind of Visual Effect. The pieces are placed in the foreground, usually above the action, lit to match the action area and with enough light to create a depth of field that covers the foreground effects piece and the background. In *Butch Cassidy and the Sundance Kid* the long shot of Butch and the Kid jumping off a cliff into a river was a glass shot. Two stunt men jumped off a scaffold into a studio backlot lake that was agitated to look like a flowing river, 12 feet from the camera a large piece of glass with a painting of both sides of the 'gorge' on it was placed to block out the scaffold and match the location. The glass and camera were tented in to control and match lighting and the camera lens focal point was positioned at the axis of the tilt so that the perspective of the painting and background would match throughout the tilt of the camera as it followed the jumpers down. In-Camera Effects shots like this save on post-production optical camera costs (not needed), but they require painting on site with the tied-off camera present to line up the painting and they must be shot when the real light matches the light and shadows in the painting.

It is easy to see that the Production Designer has the responsibility to help plan and execute these elements of the motion picture environment. Coordination with the built environment or locations is vital. A Production Designer needs to be knowledge-able of all the techniques and ready to suggest to the Director and Producer solutions to the design of a film. Special Effects can save costs and often are the only way to solve story telling problems. It is the Production Designer's job to take the lead.

Special Effects (SPFX, FX), Special Visual Effects (VFX), Computer-Generated Images (CGI) Today

Today most effects beyond the physical effects have gone digital. The possibilities of solving problems in ever expanding ways and the execution of the solutions to those problems have grown exponentially.

Like traditional Visual Effects, live action 'footage' is integrated with realistic artificial imagery to make the shot. Currently this type of Effects Work is referred to as VFX, Visual Effects. When the first explorations into solving visual problems with computers were made, this work was called CGI. Computer-Generated Images. The terms basically mean the same thing.

The digital solutions to effects shots are based on the same methods of basic analog solutions. The images to be 'matted in' created by artists doing 'digital paintings' are blended with the live action shots using computer-generated techniques instead of optical techniques. The physics and artistry are still the same only now the physics and artistry are virtual. Perspective, composition, color, atmosphere and editing are still part of the problem solving, 3D environments depicted on a 2D screen have basically the same problems and solutions whether they are digital or analog.

When we first started venturing into the digital world the solutions to problems were only partial. In *Batman Returns* a miniature graveyard was filmed, and in a separate blue screen shot actors were filmed. The film was loaded into a laser scanner and each frame was scanned onto magnetic tape. The tape was fed into a computer and the composite was made by a digital artist. The composited image was loaded back into the scanner and transferred onto film that was edited into the movie.

In *Back to the Future II* the dolly, pan, tilt and zoom of a motion controlled camera were tracked by computers and the camera moves could be repeated exactly to capture the same actor playing different parts in the same scene. The final composites of these shots were done digitally on computers. This was one step beyond the first *Star Wars* shots that were photographed with motion control cameras and composited photographically on optical cameras.

One of the advantages of digital visual effects is that the camera no longer needs to be stationary. A program called Match Move or other similar programs can track every tiny or major move the camera that's following the main action takes. whatever needs to be matted in; an actor's face on a stuntman, a truck rolling through the air, an ape swinging on a vine, a passing cityscape or an ocean liner passing by, can follow the exposure, focus and atmosphere in relative perspective to the main shot. There are so many of these kind of shots in the current *Star Wars* movies that you can't keep track of them. But that's the point, you should be so involved in the story that you don't notice. In retrospect if you ask yourself how did they do that? The answer today is, most likely it was VFX, CGI, Digital or Computer Imaging. It all means the same thing and the most often used 'official' terms are VFX, Visual Effects or Special Effects. The traditional physical effects that weren't optical effects or visual effects are now often called Mechanical Effects or Physical Effects to distinguish them.

It is very common now to build parts of sets and back them with green screen while shooting and then add to the sets digitally. The digital artists need to know architecture and are supervised by the Production Designer. The locations can be enhanced the same way. Lucas Film coined the words SET EXTENSIONS to describe this process. At first it was common to see this done without moving the camera, similar to a traditional matte shot and sometimes without green screen. In the movie *Primal Fear*, the church next to the rectory was entirely a digital construction, using the top of an existing foreground wall for a matte line. The houses on location in *Mother* and in *Saving Mr. Banks* were sets whose second floors and roofs were entirely digital. Digital Set Extensions are common in period films. Buckingham Palace in *Darkest Hour* and in the TV series *The Crown* are mostly Set Extensions. Everything beyond the first two blocks of the New York Street set in Peter Jackson's *King Kong* and in *Fantastic Beasts and Where to Find Them* is a Digital Set Extension—the rest of the city as far as you can see. Much of the Hospital Ship you see in *Dunkirk* and the Pier it is tied to are Digital Extensions of the set.

Some movies are almost entirely digital, all the environment and all the animals in the 2016 version of *Jungle Book* are digital. It is beautifully done and extremely well 'shot'. Even though the entire movie was made in Los Angeles, while I was watching the movie I believed that I was in a Central Indian Forest and that the animals could really talk and sing. The live actor worked in a neutral space in a sound stage with some set elements like those you might find on a blue screen set. The Director and his crew had to have a very good idea where everything in the virtual world was and exactly how it related to the actor's performance. The Production Designer is responsible for the designed virtual environment and must be actively involved in helping the Director and the actors find their way around the digital world.

Motion Capture Movie Making is much the same kind of problem solving that was used in *Jungle Book* but it is at first much more abstract and eventually much more detail oriented. The big difference is that the actors are digitally rendered too. The actor's physical performance, their voice and their facial expressions are 'captured' by camera-like sensors and their performance is digitally inserted into the virtual world. The biggest difficulty in motion capture is orienting the movie crew to the virtual environment. Some Directors, Actors and Production Designers can visualize the cinematic sequences and deal with the abstract quite well. Their job is to make it all clear for the rest of the crew. Great concept sketches, set models and storyboards are required to help the whole crew 'see' what is happening in the capture space. Production Designers must accurately render the sets in digital 3D, design the props and set elements the actors interact with and create accurate spotting plans that tell where the action and set pieces are within the capture space. The idea is to place anything physical, set pieces or an actor's action, exactly where they belong in the 3D virtual environment. The enterprise may seem too complicated, but two big factors make it worth developing. You only need to 'shoot' master shots because all the following breakdown shots can be found in the digital world of the master. 'Shooting' time (capturing time) with the full crew is cut in half. Animation time of the final compositing (the resolution of the performances) is cut in half because the actors provide the basic animation from their captured performances.

All motion capture movies require that you build the entire world behind the actors. That is also true for most large scale action pictures today. Production Designers must create the 'universe' of these films. We can't build the entire environment pixel by pixel, there's not enough time or money for that. We must resort to old cinematic tricks to create the digital world. CGI mattes, CGI cut-outs, CGI backings and CGI repetition of architectural elements and action make it possible. We used to make molded fiberglass pieces of buildings so they could be repeated often and fill the set backgrounds. The same can be done digitally and on a much grander scale. Entire buildings, city blocks, mountains and huge chunks of forest can be repeated as much as we want. Programs have been developed to randomly vary the elements and diminish the detail (and computing space) to build vast areas of the far background and not show a repetitive pattern. We used to photograph the same 200 hundred costumed extras at different places in our fields or plazas and composite them to make armies or mobs. The same thing can be done digitally. In the movie *Beowulf* a dozen actors were captured fighting with different medieval weapons. The captured action was rendered completely for the foreground, then randomly altered (by computer program), doubled and reduced in detail for the immediate background, doubled and reduced in detail for the next level and so-on until the screen was filled with two armies engaged on a field of battle. The same was done for B-24s in *Unbroken* and a giant fleet of ships in *Flag of Our Fathers* and all the spacecraft in the latest Star Wars movies. No miniatures in large water tanks or in front of motion control cameras anymore.

New CGI cinematic tricks are being invented at a rapid pace. The idea of 2-and-a-half-D was invented recently: projecting 2D images onto 3D shapes to quickly develop a background. Also, there is the notion of 'slaving' a cut-out 2D 'backing' to a virtual camera so that it always faces the camera no matter where the camera moves. Production Designers need to be constantly learning how their designed environments can be 'built'.

The majority of animated movies are completely CGI. Production Designers creating the settings will apply most of the VFX techniques that have been discussed in this essay.

Most medium and large scale movies today apply CGI or VFX solutions to some or all of their visual problems. 19th Century Warships, and the water that they are in, the locomotive and trestle in, *The Orient Express*, all the cars and trucks that super heroes toss around and buildings they knock down are digital. Although many of the exotic places in *Star Wars* movies are real with substantial sets built in them, almost their entire worlds are digital. Explosions, breaking glass and crashing vehicles are more likely to be CGI. The two *Blade Runner* Movies are great to compare, The first one made in 1981 uses Matte Shots, Miniatures, Blue Screen and other traditional effects and optical effects. *Blade Runner 2049*, made in 2016 and 2017, is filled almost entirely with digital environments and vehicles beyond the built portions of sets. Sometimes the actors perform in a complete digital environment and they need the concept art and possibly scale models of the sets provided by the Production Designer to understand where they are and what they are looking at.

Production Designers today need to have a complete knowledge of how digital sets are designed and integrated with the action and the actors. The approach to creating the movie environment today uses a lot of traditional thinking and an understanding of traditional visual effects. After all it is still telling stories in the way we have always done. But we need great concept artists and great digital environment designers and great VFX experts in our departments to help tell the story, and we must be able to understand what they can do and how they do it.

There are many movie and television shows that still use traditional effects as well as CGI or VFX. Sometimes for the economy and sometimes because the Director wants to use traditional effects only because that's his style. There is lots of literature exploring Special Effects and many websites exploring VFX. Make yourself knowledgeable.

—Article by Norm Newberry.

Stunts

One Producer liked to say he absolutely *hated* stunts, because there was always the possibility that something could go terribly wrong, involving the safety of one or more crew members.

On the morning of a stunt where two main characters were to 'bungee-jump' off of a bridge (we used the famous one in Pasadena with the arches), this Producer was nervous and NOT, for once, concerned with the clock.

The Stunt Coordinators were all there, talking the actors through the *simplicity* of the jump. There were inflatables on the ground for landing, cushioning the drop, should any cord accidentally malfunction (break).

It seemed a fairly simple, straightforward stunt; both male characters were confident they could do the jump, no problem. They were in costume and full bungee-cord harness, ready to go.

The sun was right, the Director was about to call action, when, at the LOUD insistence of this Producer, **a 'practice take' was requested**.

Frustrated by the delay, discussions about just exactly 'how' to do this 'practice take' followed; who should do the practice take? Stand-ins? Extras? How about a watermelon? Or, should a stunt guy go off the bridge first, to show how *easy* this was? (not the same weight).

The Producer was concerned about safety; **no human being should jump off the bridge before a test run first**.

The Stunt Coordinator hit on the idea of *sandbags*; the exact same weight as one of the actors, wrapped in the same bungee cords they planned to use in the scene.

This compromise was agreed to by the Producer and quickly put into action (sandbags had to be found; another delay).

Figure 13.10 Stunts, Sidney Lumet and crew watch in fear, *Child's Play* (1972)

While the crew waited impatiently, concerned about losing the sunlight and the time to make the day's shots, several sandbags were grudgingly wrapped in bungee cords.

Nearly an hour later the moment arrived at last; we were ready for the 'practice take'. The entire crew was standing below the bridge, watching.

The Director called 'action' and the sandbags were thrown over the railing of the bridge ... **and promptly bounced back up UNDERNEATH the concrete structure of the bridge!**

The actor's heads would have been crushed.

The crew was silent.

And that's why most Producers insist on rehearsals and practice takes before any stunts.

Stunts require safety meetings, preparation and professionals ... as well as caution!

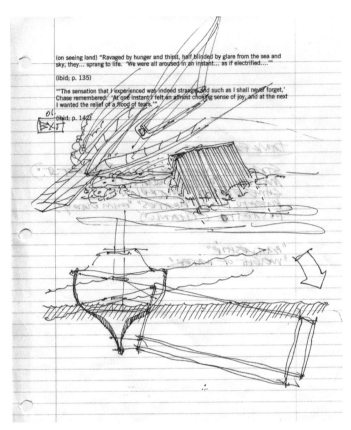

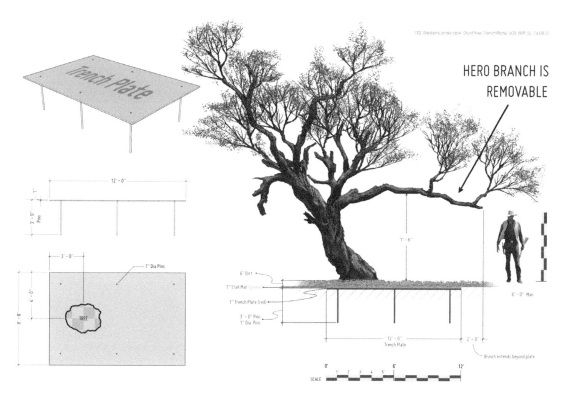

Figure 13.12 Stunt tree rig, Western location (design – before)

Figure 13.13 Stunt tree scene, Western location (actual realization - after)

Figure 13.14 Water tank set, Sony Stage, *Hail, Caesar!*

Figure 13.15 Scarlett Johansson swimming in tank set, *Hail, Caesar!*

The following are additional images illustrating practical effects on location:

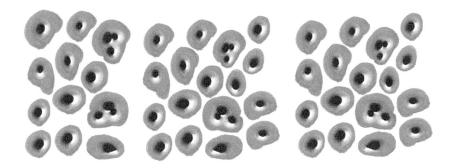

Figure 13.16 *The Kingdom*, photoshop bullet hits (for application)

Figure 13.17 *The Kingdom*, special FX explosion (practical)

Figure 13.18 Practical location/green screen for *Patriots Day* (before)

Figure 13.19 Green screen for *Patriots Day* (after)

Figure 13.20 *Exodus: Gods and Kings*, green screen set on location and finished shot

THE BOOK OF EXODUS   CONCEPT ART / VFX

0012_Ext_Temple of Sekhmet_Leaving for Battle_Set Extension_view1_sc5

Figure 13.21 *Interstellar*, ranger spacecraft on stage (surrounded by white 'CYC' for digital environment)

CHAPTER 14

Lighting/Cinematography Department

Cinematography is simply 'sculpting with light'; consciously choosing and placing lights and creating shadows.

Lighting is the craft of *thoughtful storytelling*, instead of simply filming with available light and just getting it recorded, for convenience.

A good Cinematographer can make anything look good, it doesn't matter what tools they use, because they have a CREATIVE MIND … and because STORY more important than equipment!

—Lee Redmond (Cinematographer, Director)

Good Cinematography is thinking visually about the environment; a Cinematographer uses **visual logic** to show accuracy and details.

A good Cinematographer's job is to *weave a thread of continuity* through each scene, *consistently*—the same as the Production Designer.

—Kenn Ferro, Director, School of Motion Pictures, Academy of Art
University (AAU) of San Francisco

The triumvirate of filmmaking is the <u>Director</u>, the <u>Production Designer</u> and the <u>Cinematographer</u>.

Together these three department heads design and create the *look and emotion of the story*.

Lee Redmond (Cinematographer, Director) grew up in the Hollywood film industry; his mother worked on *Gone With the Wind* as an Illustrator, his grandfather was the first-ever Special Effects man in the early days of filmmaking, working on *King Kong*, and his father continued in the business, working in effects, underwater filming (*Sea Hunt*) and progressing to Vice President of the Ivan Tors Production Company.

Lee studied photography AND art before becoming a Cinematographer; an excellent foundation for lighting design.

As Lee relates:

… back in the day, cameras didn't move; Cinematographers <u>used a lot of light</u> (sunlight); later, the German silent films progressed to <u>using lights and shadows</u>.

In the mid-thirties, lighting got to be exquisite (*Rebecca, Citizen Kane*), using *chiaroscuro* (bold and dramatic contrast of dark and light), or lights and darks to define the scenes.

Technicolour technicians were used on set, resulting in over-lit, super-bright images. The ART of lighting took a hit for separating and showing <u>depth</u>, for color.

Cinematographers <u>fought</u> for lighting with shadows.

Then, in the '70s and '80s, Vittorio Storaro (*author: *Writing With Light*) emerged, producing *really good* artistic lighting (Apocalypse Now, *Last Tango in Paris*).

Today, it's a digital world; cameras are more sensitive to light, producing *realism*, and we've lost the quality of <u>'sculpting with light'</u>.

Digital filmmakers are no longer using light to push <u>story</u>; they're just using light for *convenience*.

—Lee Redmond (Cinematographer, Director)

<u>Lighting, consciously choosing and placing lights and creating shadows, is the craft of thoughtful storytelling.</u>

This is different than simply 'filming with whatever light is available and getting it recorded'.

Camera operating is falling apart in movies today, because 'gear heads' (technical operators) are not used anymore. 'Gearheads' control the camera … *<u>this is not taught anymore</u>*!

Digital is not a physical medium; it's a new language developed for film that comes with a new freedom (life does not come with a 'cut').

Digital has a great 'dynamic range', and as the digital world has gotten better, it's gotten closer to film.

Cinematography is in a low spot right now because of digital … *<u>they are not lighting to support the story</u>*.

Currently, digital has come to be working with 'found light' (available light), because it's *easy* and *fast*—but *<u>you can't count on 'available light'</u>*! Available light (sunlight) moves constantly, changes regularly, and cannot be reproduced.

Figure 14.1 *Birdman*, dressing room set, lighting

Figure 14.2 *ET*, cine effects on set

Fast and convenient is 'documentary style', *not ART*.

You couldn't shoot a picture like *Double Indemnity* on digital.

The point to good or even great Cinematography is NOT for convenience! 'Good enough' is not the point.

STORY is EVERYTHING!

Story is more important than the equipment.

Most good DP's (Cinematographers) are on the Production Designer's side … they like:

- Compass directions (for determining sun and shadows)
- Distance (for cables, equipment needs, etc.)
- Scale/size
- Volume (for smoke)
- Plot plans of locations containing facts.

Good Production Designers ***give the Cinematographer something to light!!!*** This could mean reflections, textures, blinds/window mullions to create shadow patterns, etc.

As always, keep STORY at the top of every discussion!

Relationship to the DP/Cinematographer

The relationship with the Cinematographer is built on *respect.*

> *Find a way to HELP them; we need each other.*
> *If the set isn't well lit, we've all wasted our time.*
>
> —Jeannine Oppewall (*LA Confidential, Pleasantville,*
> *Catch Me If You Can, Seabiscuit*)

As Production Designers, it's up to us to **GIVE THE DP** (or Cinematographer) **SOMETHING TO LIGHT!!!**

The most important aspect of a set lighting discussion is, 'where, exactly, is the camera in relation to the set, and what are we seeing?'

It is up to the Production Designer to offer the ability and access to lighting sets.

Make use of TEXTURES, LAYERS, SOURCES, OPPORTUNITIES … give thought to how your sets will look when lit!

Think about reflections, what might create beautiful shadows, add dimension to your sets.

In the pre-production phase, be sure to meet with the Cinematographer to discuss:

- Practicals
- Texture
- Colour
- Size of sets (room for their lights).

---

* *Give the Cine crew enough room for their equipment*; accommodate/hide cords and cables; and ***give plenty of 'practicals'*** (fireplace, sconces, chandeliers, etc.)

Also to be discussed:

- Scale, distance, direction on compass; N, S, E, or W of locations (for the sun source)
- Facts; volume (for smoke effect)
- Offer them plot plans with as many facts and details as you can provide.

<u>ALWAYS KEEP STORY AT THE TOP OF EVERY LIST AND DISCUSSION!</u>

Figure 14.3 *The Adventures of Robin Hood*, Technicolor frame

BELOW: Figure 14.4 *The Adventures of Robin Hood* (1938), stage set

BOTTOM RIGHT: Figure 14.5 *The Adventures of Robin Hood* (1938), stage set/Technicolor camera. A heavy-duty crane angles into the set with a three-strip Technicolor camera while filming the grand banquet hall scene (courtesy of Technicolor).

Figure 14.6 *The Kingdom* set, walls painted gloss for reflective effect

It is wise to include the Cinematographer early on. We have to be cognizant of their job at all times; ceilings can't be too low, window designs deserve special attention, and the overall space needs to be addressed, first in broad terms and then in more specific detail.

Always keep them in the loop, share visuals and materials with them, embrace their images and input.

Together, the two of you are trying to figure out the VISUAL VOCABULARY for the project. Talk all the time!

Lighting is technical, so bringing the technical issues to the conversation will empower each department, and can often lead to the unexpected.

Ask: 'How will you light this?' and begin the collaboration.

Good Cinematography is 'thinking visually about the environment'. Good Production Design provides the environment.

> Build a set not just for how it looks, but for how it works.
> —Nelson Coates (*Flight, 50 Shades of Grey, Murder at 1600, Runaway Jury*)

For the movie *Runaway Jury*, Nelson Coates designed the courtroom set *specifically* for the Cinematographer and ease of the production crew.

Some examples:

- The jury box was designed and built on a wagon (wheels), for ease of 'moving to camera'
- The stained-glass windows were all hinged, for ease of lighting and to eliminate reflections
- Walls were designed on wagons (wheels) to move in and out quickly, and to accommodate cranes
- Panels within the woodwork were designed to open for cables
- The floor pattern was designed for ease of furniture placement.

Figure 14.7 *Hail, Caesar! stage*, dance

Figure 14.8 Stage, water, submarine

Try to do things with your design to HELP the Cinematographer and lighting crew.

Helping everyone makes each of you look better!

When the Cinematographer arrives, _the relationship between the Cinematographer and the Director becomes the most important relationship on the film_; this is the heart of the film.

Because of this crucial dynamic, **_Production Designers must cultivate good working relationships with both the Director and Cinematographer_**.

The magic occurs when imagination meets the practical realities of filmmaking.

Bill Ross (**_Columbo, Mission Impossible_** (TV)) was a Production Designer who was very proud of his 'honorary union card' in the Cinematographer's union, Local # 600.It was given to him unanimously by crew members after years of designing sets with lighting considerations in mind.

Bill often told the story of a set he once built for a _Mission Impossible_ (TV show) episode, which could have been a disaster if it wasn't for the Cinematographer and lighting crew to save him.

The set was to take place in Africa. Bill's challenge was to build a large office set on a California sound stage that would look and feel like we were in Africa. Several important African dignitaries were to meet with one of the _Mission Impossible_ crew and play the scene.

In doing his research, Bill found that African Zebra wood would be just the right material to use for the walls of the set, giving the impression of wealth and exotic location at once.

The set was built and dressed, beautifully. When the actors arrived, the entire cast was African—including the _Mission Impossible_ star, Greg Morris!

With dark brown walls and dark brown skin tones, the Cinematographer was presented with a definite problem. Rising to the occasion, they achieved success by highlighting the walls instead of the actors, and by collaborating with Wardrobe and set dressing for lighter coloured garments and several more 'practical' lights on set.

Bill had made the mistake of seizing on what seemed a good design idea at the time, but ended up near-disaster for the Cinematographer. Collaboration is ALWAYS necessary, no matter how seasoned the team may be!

Bill Ross had a great sense of humour, and told this story often with great delight; he had nothing but respect for the Cinematographer and their team. They knew this, and were happy to work with him.

Another reason for his honorary Union card in the Lighting Union (Local #600) is because when Bill designed his sets, he **always** allowed for the placement of lights and for the hiding of cables, mounts, and supports, even and especially on locations. He considered their team as part of his own, and the respect was noticed and appreciated.

For one _Columbo_ episode, he designed a special type of 'pilaster' (1/2 column) that was spring-loaded, top and bottom, to fit between the ceiling and floor of an office building on location. These were open at the back, to hide and 'cover' the cords and cables that the Cinematographer would need to light the cavernous space.

These 1/2 columns were painted to match the location walls and could be moved to camera and placed anywhere; a win-win for both departments!

> If there is no solution, there is no problem.
>
> —Philippe Rousselot, Cinematographer, *Peacock*

Figure 14.9 *Hail, Caesar!* period backlot lighting (Warner Brothers)

This type of consideration for fellow departments goes beyond 'collaboration'; it shows a true understanding and empathy for what's needed to produce the optimum results on the project.

Bill thought of lighting as one of the most important elements of his sets. He designed lots of windows whenever possible and appropriate, to allow for different lighting effects such as shadow branches outside the windows, blowing curtains inside the windows, and venetian blinds creating interesting patterns (also to control the amount of light coming through).

He thought of including 'practicals' (lamps, sconces, chandeliers, etc.) as much as possible, and often said 'think of what you need, and then triple it'!

He looked for and found creative ways to *allow* for lighting opportunities, such as fireplaces, open 'fretwork', corbels or gingerbread panels (architectural term for carved wooden details), recessed lighting and picture lamps over paintings or on bookshelves.

The obvious fish tanks allow lighting opportunities that, in the case of The *Graduate* movie, may even suggest the framing and filming of a scene, which might not have been in the script.

On the other hand, a lack of consideration for the lighting department can be disastrous; as was the case when a Production Designer built a beautiful Victorian home on stage, with sweeping staircase and different floor levels—the Cinematographer had a fit, because he had no place to put his lights and the intricate woodwork, railings, and detailing, and different floor levels created problems with unwanted shadows on the actor's faces as well as the dolly track.

Figure **14.10** *Age of Innocence*, dolly track

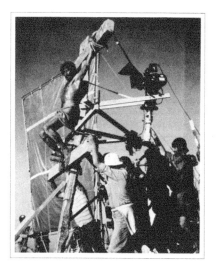

Figure **14.11** *The Last Temptation of Christ*, Scorsese

Good Production Design is so much more than design! It is considering everything about the setting in which the story takes place, and creating a back-story for the setting, like an actor does for his character.

This means the thought and attention to every aspect of the set, at every time of day or night, mood, season, time period, location, and so on, and must appear *appropriate* and *naturally correct* and *interesting*, all at the same time!

Figure 14.12 *Christine*
(1983), car camera rig

Figure 14.13 *Last Action
Hero*, Shotmaker camera
rig

The Warren Beatty *Dick Tracy* movie, designed by Dick Sylbert on Universal's backlot, is a perfect example of what can happen when the Art Department and the Cinematography/lighting departments don't communicate or see eye to eye …

Flawlessly designed sets, costumes and make-up were completely thrown off by the use of a 'cartoon', or primary, lighting colour palette.

Figure 14.14 *Sleepers,* 360° dolly track

In theory, they were all on the same page using the same colours, but the coloured lighting ended up negating the effect they were going for.

Together, ideally, the PD and the Cinematographer should 'weave a thread of continuity' through each scene, using **visual logic**.

This begins with a **design brief**, *approved by the Director*, which should include:

- **Tone/approach** (gritty vs slick, etc.)
- Colour palette
- Seasons
- Locale (New England, the South, Europe, etc.)
- Time period
- Mood/feeling (cold, gloomy, etc.).

Later, you can get into specifics of each character, as Hitchcock liked to do (lead character always wears green, thief always smokes, etc.)—these details **enhance the story and the characters as well as the look of the shoot**. They can be fun, and often create memorable scenes.

Story always comes first. The story must be at the top of everyone's list, all the time. Cinematography/lighting is the craft of *thoughtful storytelling*, instead of just using 'found light' or 'available light' and simply recording the action (this is documentary style). Consciously choosing and placing lights and creating shadows and a deliberate

<u>atmosphere is Cinematography at its highest form</u>. *A good Production Designer can help this process by communicating mood, colours, textures and bringing them all together.*

These two departments, together, create EMOTION for the scene.

Without a word of dialogue, emotion is evident and palpable: REAL.

Figure 14.15 *Gravity*, set piece with lighting

Figure 14.16 *Life of Pi*, Production Designer David Gropman. A bioluminescent glow of marine phosphorescence surrounds the raft and lifeboat during a sequence in the film that came to be called 'tiger vision'.

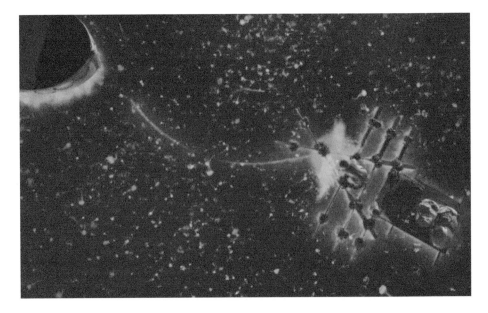

Films for Reference

Road to Perdition (Connie Hall, dark, candle-lit)
Citizen Kane (chiaroscuro/lights and darks, shadows to save $ on sets)
Double Indemnity (moody, dark, black and white, height contrast)
Avalon (firework reflections in puddle, DP shopped for chandelier with PD for weeks)
Hail, Caesar! (mentioned by several DPs … range, quality, exquisite lighting … respect!)

There is a term used in the industry to describe that *perfect glow of sunset* that is every Cinematographer's dream to capture—it's that brief time of day when everything is bathed in warm light, and lasts for less than an hour: it's called **MAGIC HOUR**.

Cinematographers check the timing of the sunset (approximate, at best), which will vary at different locations.

Often, the exact angle of a sunset or sunrise shot related to the elements of a set needs to be determined by the Production Designer, using sun charts and location data for the scheduled day of a shoot.

On occasion, a Cinematographer may need afternoon shadows or natural backlight for a scene. You must spot your set or recommend a time to shoot the scene to help accomplish the shot. On the film, *The Best Little Whore House in Texas*, Art Director Norm Newberry used a county road map and the sun chart in Architectural Graphics Standards to find the location for this sunset shot (see Figure 14.20):

A favourite trick used by old-school Cinematographers to gauge the amount of time and light remaining was shared with me years ago on a set in Malibu:

> Look out at the horizon, then hold your fingers up parallel to the horizon, first finger at the bottom of the sun.
>
> The number of fingers you have between the bottom of the sun and the horizon will tell you how much time you have left to shoot before sunset (each finger equals 5 minutes).
>
> In other words, if you can fit four fingers from the bottom of the sun to the horizon, you have 20 minutes until sunset!

Works every time, no matter where you are.

On Tech/Digital

The language of film is always evolving.

There is a new FREEDOM coming with digital changes.

Digital is not a physical medium, as film was; it's lighter and faster, and can be moved in ways you couldn't dream of ten years ago.

Digital doesn't 'stop the energy of the circus' (the film crew).

In the digital world, there are no 'CUTS'—and life doesn't have a 'cut'; it's a new language developed for film.

Digital cameras are more sensitive to light. They are lighter and more portable.

Figure 14.17 *The Best Little Whore House in Texas*, sunset shot planned and spotted by Art Director Norm Newberry

Source: Courtesy of Norm Newberry

Figure 14.18 *Magic Hour*, marina

Digital has REALISM, but it has *lost the character of sculpting with light*. Digital has great 'dynamic range'—as the digital world has gotten better, it's gotten closer to film. That doesn't mean it's being used WELL … the equipment doesn't make the project better— STORY STILL HAS TO COME FIRST!!!

Digital has a different way of seeing; we need to understand it *and work with it*; in other words, we need to help the Cinematographer 'sculpt with light'.

Because to make it look good, you still have to light it!!!

In the digital world, all too often Cinematographers are not using light to *push the story*; they are just using light for convenience. You can't count on 'available light'; it won't be there tomorrow!

You can't try to shoot in 'real time'—which may be fast and convenient but it looks like 'found light', as in documentaries.

It's time to embrace digital as its own medium, not trying to make it look like film.

Both mediums are best when used HONESTLY.

As always, STORY **is more important than equipment!**

CHAPTER 15

Production Meetings and Changes

Nothing ever goes the way the budget or the schedule says it will ... you make the movie on how clever you are and by fixing whatever is wrong.

—Norm Newberry (*Avatar, The River, Ghost Story, Polar Express, The Mask*)

Changes

Learning to anticipate what <u>might</u> go wrong and planning for it is a requirement for every Production Designer.

Efficient planning ahead of time for changes and having OPTIONS to offer for consideration in the event of unavoidable changes is the mark of the true professional.

Maintaining passion, excitement, and enthusiasm (positivity) is a crucial skill for when the inevitable happens; some sort of CHANGE to the already approved—sometimes built-plan.

The Production Designer is responsible for cheerful, efficient flexibility ... most often to simply *encourage* the team when an unexpected 'curve ball' comes their way.

Even if money has been spent and time has been committed, we are responsible for the look of the film under any conditions, and it falls to us to confidently convince the team that the 'alternate' will be *just as successful*, if not more so, than the original.

When a change occurs on a production, one of the first cases made is to the Production Designer; because WE are responsible for the look of the film and for providing something to shoot!

By the way, a change doesn't always mean a loss of location or set; it may also involve and ADDED scene and/or sets.

An example would be if mid-shoot, the Director/Producer/Writer decide that they need to add a scene or a few 'simple' shots by tomorrow.

The call comes around 10:00 pm to the Production Designer: 'We need a new set by tomorrow morning; what can you have ready to shoot?'

Thinking on your feet is another critical skill of the Production Designer.

We are often asked to make quick decisions like this, at a moment's notice, often involving large amounts of money and impacting the entire cast and crew.

Confidence and a clear understanding of the repercussions to each department that your decision will affect will help you to articulate time, costs, and feasibility.

Continuing to use the example of the 'last-minute added set', with less than 24 hours' 'turnaround' reduces the options to which walls or flats are available for a quick paint job, and an assessment of the story action happening in the set; is a door required, for entrances and/or exits? Will we need a backup wall, or return, or corridor? Window(s)? If so, what type of backing outside the window? Any greens? Special lighting? Tone of the scene?

Because we design for the story (and characters), we need answers and information before we can simply 'put up a set'. These answers help us to estimate the costs involved, which we'll be asked to 'guesstimate' immediately before the added set is approved.

Knowing and estimating time and materials should become second nature, with experience.

Figure 15.1 Ron Howard plus producing partner Brian Glazer on set of *How the Grinch Stole Christmas* (2000)

Of course, Production is aware this is a 'rush job', and will cost more, accordingly.

Once approved (usually over the same phone call, in a short discussion and a matter of minutes), the added set must be arranged, ASAP.

The Production Designer's first call is to the Construction Coordinator; walls and logistics are discussed, carpenters and painters are called in (yes, the night before the shoot), and the Production Designer must drive to the stage to select paint colours and 'spot the set', placing doors and windows—if any—according to how the new scene might best be filmed.

The second call the Production Designer makes is to the Set Decorator; they must discuss colour palette and furnishings, to include: artwork, practical lamps, window treatments, rugs, pillows, plants, etc., and the two departments confirm an understanding of the tone (action) of the added scene. Any props, if necessary, will be discussed and the Set Decorator will usually communicate with the Prop Master. Every department affected has a crew to alert, assign call times and tasks, and generally make them aware of the *approved change in the schedule tomorrow*, and how all will be affected.

The Production Designer may even select a few camera angles for the Director, to take advantage of the best views of set, thoughtfully offering options to the Director who will not be familiar with this 'surprise' set, and will not have had an opportunity to prepare his blocking and/or lighting.

In a matter of hours, the 'added scene/set' is in the works, with each department making cost adjustments to their budgets, which the Producer will ask for immediately if not sooner!

Production Meetings

Production meetings are your opportunity to go through the entire script together with the Director and each department head. The First Assistant Director runs the production meeting and, often, it is the only time you will see the Studio VPs on location.

It is probably the ONLY time that you will all be together in the same room, with full access to the Director's attention. Be selective in the questions you ask; show your priorities and have respect for everyone's time. There is never enough time to cover everything.

Each department has specifics necessary to ask the Director, and you have the opportunity to learn an incredible amount of information, just by listening!

The meetings usually last about 2 hours or more (one went on for a day and a half!), and you do not want to miss anything!

No matter how busy you are, ***never miss these all-important meetings!*** You are a department head, and expected to be there for questions, solutions, suggestions, and answers.

These meetings are also your opportunity to hear from every department regarding the shoot. This information is valuable and may not be repeated: take notes and pay attention!

The production meeting is the perfect time to hand out the Director's plans of your sets, any approved storyboards that have been prepared, in addition to approved signs and logos for wardrobe, transportation, etc.

Visuals from your department are a treat; often, they will mark the first time many of the production team will get to see what is being planned to film, including colours, locations, size, and scale of sets, and any speciality scenes (custom vehicles, props, architectural designs, etc.).

This is your moment to shine!

Be prepared to show everything you and the Director and Cinematographer have discussed, visually, for the shoot. Copies can be made later; this meeting is for discussion and information purposes, and YOUR VISUALS ARE KEY to understanding!

Also be prepared to answer questions about sets, timing, access to locations.

The Director will go through the script page by page, scene by scene, and cover all details and requirements, answer any questions and generally 'lay out their vision' for the show at this meeting.

Occasionally, there will be a 'side meeting', where the Director decides to meet with a department head later, at another time, so as not to waste the entire company's time (such as a stunt, wardrobe issue, or any special effects).

In the past, a movie wasn't started and crewed up until it was greenly by the studio; today, some shows aren't greenly until weeks into principal photography.

Time is so short in prep these days, often a lot of locations, sets, and even the script haven't all been worked out yet … a lot of TBD. You just have to stay professional and 'go with the flow'.

Sometimes, an important set or location will not yet be 'locked'; in this case, always try to have a Plan B ready, just in case.

Production Meetings

Production meetings are the only group meetings that take place before the episode or project begins, and these meetings are the only time when ALL department heads are present. The Director will go through the script, page by page and scene by scene, with the help of the First AD (Assistant Director). They will cover all details and requirements and answer any questions. This process is a chance to learn about the Director's vision for the show so that everyone understands what the production will attempt to achieve. Any and all-important questions should be asked and answered, and everyone learns together about how the project is to be filmed and what the plans are for the entire shoot.

Note the following:

- Occasionally, there will be an area marked **TBD** (to be determined); in this case, always have a backup plan, just in case the primary plan isn't determined in time.
- The **shooting schedule** (prepared by the first AD, listing dates, times, and locations for every scene in the script) will be presented to all departments at this meeting.
- During a production meeting, a Director may call separate **side meetings** with chosen departments, to be held at another time. This is to avoid wasting time on department specifics and to keep the overall script meeting moving.

Production meetings are your opportunity to hear from every department regarding the shoot. Everyone will have questions for you (the Production Designer) specific to their own department needs. The meetings will last approximately two hours (or more) and are filled with essential information. You *never* want to miss a production meeting!

The production meeting is the perfect time for you, as head of the Art Department, to hand out a set of **Director's plans** for all of the **sets**, as well as any **storyboards** and approved **signs and logos** that are ready at the time of the meeting. Even if the other departments don't use them, you have 'covered' yourself (by informing them of all the information) in case any future issues or questions arise about your sets.

After the meeting, you will move quickly into principal photography.

Good luck!

Changes

'There are no problems, only opportunities …'

This is a favourite quote among professionals in the business, because it is one of the best attitudes you can have.

Changes happen regularly and on a daily basis; your ability to react <u>calmly</u> and <u>positively</u> to any sudden alteration regarding the project you are working on will earn you a reputation for being *solutions-oriented* and a *team player;* you will be respected and appreciated for this.

Amateurs may whine and complain, throw tantrums and generally lower morale for everyone; *decide ahead of time that you will be a mature professional!*

Accept changes gracefully and even cheerfully; this is *leadership*.

It's up to you to set the tone. Your team and the entire production company are watching and paying attention to your flexibility and manners as well as your style.

This isn't the time to look for or place blame; when changes occur, they affect EVERYONE, some more than others. Changes are never easy, which makes this skill even more desirable if you want to stand out and define your reputation for success.

You, as the Production Designer and head of the Art Department, are their leader; you can inspire your team to 'make it happen'.

Sometimes, the end result may even turn out to be better!

Changes and difficulties <u>bring out the best in a leader more quickly than anything else</u>.

It's easy to lead when all runs smoothly and according to plan!

But when the occasional bump in the road occurs, this is when the *true professionals* are separated from the wannabes.

Changes come often and should be expected.

You can't always plan something to go wrong, but in case it does, always have a 'plan B' ready!

Being prepared with options shows <u>maturity</u> and <u>competence</u>.

You will impress your colleagues with your ingenuity and support, and your attitude will speak volumes about your character. No one wants the boss who rants and raves or flies off the handle in anger; we all respond better to encouragement, challenge, and creativity.

You will become the hero of the hour if, instead of panic and complaints, you offer a viable suggestion to actually help the company over the rough patch.

Again, <u>you are building your reputation every day</u>.

As head of the Art Department, you set the tone for everyone. Determine to be a good leader and a supportive colleague, as well as a great communicator and collaborator right from the start and beginning of every job.

The way that you handle changes and unexpected surprises matters more than you think; remember, your team is looking to YOU for their example.

One area that changes really affect is the budget.

Often, the money has been spent on a set or location, and a major change can require production and/or studio approval along with a substantial sum of money added to the budget, sometimes called an 'approved overage'.

Some of the typical changes that may come your way could be anything from *'we have a problem; the writers have added another set for this scene, & we need to shoot it tomorrow'*—can you make it happen?

Or *'we had to change the schedule due to the lead actor's availability, and we now need the BIG set a week earlier'*—is it possible?

Or, *'the giant space station set has now been changed to an underwater cave … how soon can you have it ready?'*

Yes, these types of changes will happen.

As a department head, you will be notified as quickly as possible, and a solution and an answer will be expected.

Take a deep breath, remain calm, and, if necessary, buy some time while you 'consult with your Construction Manager' … no matter how frustrated or upset you may feel inside, never let it show!

This is your job; once filming begins on a project, it is up to you as Production Designer to make sure the shooting company always has a place to film, every day! This includes **cover sets** for rain or bad weather, **emergency 'swing' sets** ready as backup for moments of 'just in case', even offering to **'re-vamp' a previous set** to adapt for the scene at hand.

Time and quick thinking will save the day, and will reveal how prepared you are as a professional Production Designer.

All you can do is to plan for the worst, celebrate the best, and expect to receive 'all of the blame and none of the credit'.

You will build a reputation as a Production Designer who is 'ready for anything and is a pleasure to work with'—who wouldn't want to hire you?!?

Never over-react to changes or curveballs in the schedule; they are part of the business, and no matter how good you are, you cannot plan for them in advance.

As an example, on one hit TV series the young female star spent her weekend in Palm Springs, only to return so sunburned that they couldn't film her!

Since the script had been written for her, she was in every scene; all of the sets, vehicles, props, wardrobe, etc. had to be scrambled at the last moment while she took the week off.

They shot a different script, forcing all departments and crews to work overtime every day that week.

All you can do is to try to be ready with a 'Plan B' for the shooting company, 'just in case'.

This means weather (cover sets), loss of a location (re-vamp an existing set?), scheduling issues, even illness of an actor.

Be prepared. Think ahead and be positive … when all around are losing their heads, keep yours! This will earn you respect and will help to build the reputation as an unflappable PD; 'nothing can throw them off their game'.

> I had to draw that damn staircase more than 25 times!!! They couldn't make up their mind, should it curve left, should it curve right, should it curve in BOTH directions … what type of railing, how far apart the spindles should be. I got so sick of it, I didn't even care to see the movie. We all felt that way. Over two years designing and re-designing a show that didn't seem it would ever get made.
>
> —Dorothea Holt Redmond, on *Gone With the Wind*

> We built most of the city sets in Europe, and were ready to film, when production decided they wanted to bring us all back to the US.
>
> We started all over and built everything again, in California. They ended up spending 3 times what those sets would have cost.
>
> —John DeCuir, Sr, on *Cleopatra*

CHAPTER 16

Strike and Wrap

No scorched-earth policy!!! Clean it up behind you and fix it anyway.
Take your own documentary photos of your sets; use available light if you have to.
Always archive your work!

—Jeannine Oppewal (*LA Confidential, Pleasantville,
Catch Me If You Can, Seabiscuit*)

To strike a set or location always takes <u>less</u> time and effort than to build and dress a set. It's always faster to break down a set or a location than it is to install; taking away is easier and simpler.

However, just because the company is finished with a set or location, doesn't mean it shouldn't be handled with care and respect.

If the flats (walls) are to be trashed, sent to the dumpster or to some environmentally safe recycling centre for materials, they still need to be handled professionally and responsibly.

This, too, is the responsibility of the Production Designer; what we design, create, build, and install, we are responsible for removing, storing, or disposing of.

Insurance and liability requirements prevent donations of used sets and set pieces to schools and theatre groups—studios don't want law suits!

What may seem like a harmless gift or donation may result in safety and health law-suits for any number of reasons; termites, bedbugs, rodents, toxic fumes (real or imagined), etc.

The accepted policy is to dispose of or strike all sets and materials only at approved facilities.

Striking a set and preserving it for re-shoots, or for a possible sequel, involves locating and reserving a proper *storage area* (Production will have input on this).

Obviously, if the set is to be preserved, it must be handled with care.

After appropriate 'reference' photos are taken, careful handling of all flats, greens, and backings is expected.

It is not uncommon in the Los Angeles area to see trucks loaded with flats and scenery heading to or from a location, neatly stacked and secured.

Flats, although built of lumber, are fragile and can become warped and even broken with careless handling. Each step of the process is critical to the care and storage of the sets—including the driving!

Hitting a pothole in the road could cost thousands of dollars if a special finish is damaged, chipped, or fractured.

Which is why those trucks, loaded with flats and scenery, on the Hollywood Freeway are driving in the slow lane, at a snail's pace … their cargo is valuable and they are treating it with respect!

It is always best to treat a location as if it were your home; some would say your *Grandmother*'s home. In other words, with a great deal of respect.

When filming on a location, for many it is simply a job, a workplace, a temporary event.

But, for the Production Designer, every location is RESPONSIBILITY.

As Production Designer, you must be aware of everything.

Any changes or alterations (including the simplest 'improvements') you wish to make must be cleared and approved with production and with the location owner.

Film sets are not built 'to code', meaning that they are *not built to construction standards*, which are meant to last. **Insurance policies will not cover your set pieces** beyond filming, so *never promise to 'leave something' at the end of the shoot.*

You do not need a lawsuit for injuries or damage!

That beautiful pier and dock you build on someone's lakefront is NOT safe for a prolonged length of time! Which is why you need to budget money to STRIKE the pier and dock, including a crew, transportation, and where it's to be stored or disposed of.

Another possibility at the end of a shoot is the need to 'fold and hold' the set. The set may need to be held for possible retakes or added scenes.

On a television series, the best pieces of a set may be saved in a 'scene dock' for eventual reuse. The labour to do that and storage costs must be considered, plus the eventual strike when the set pieces are no longer needed.

Budgeting for strike is something to be learned with experience.

The best way, when you are just starting out, is to **imagine having to dismantle everything yourself**.

Imagine you must:

- Load it
- Transport it, and then
- Unload it again, and finally
- Drive back to the studio or home base.

This process will help you to gauge whether two men are needed or a larger crew, what size truck or transportation vehicle(s) will be needed, and roughly how much time it will take to accomplish the strike *in its entirety (including travel)*.

In the feature world, the Construction Coordinator usually budgets for strike as **a percentage of the construction costs**. Some sets are held for possible re-shoots and some sets are demolished. Location sets are usually brought back to original conditions *unless agreements are made beforehand* to leave what work has been done.

Many Production Designers will try to see if the location will keep the colours they paint, as it saves time and money, and most of the time is an improvement over the existing colours.

Do not overlook the clean-up crew in your strike budget!

Man-hours are budgeted for the entire time a crew is working; your Construction Coordinator is more familiar with each department's wages, per hour and per day (painters, wallpapers, carpenters, labourers), and which vehicles and drivers must be added as well.

Often, Production Designers discuss the strike budget with their construction coordinator to confirm costs and timeframe.

After a while, you will learn by experience how long things will take to build, set up, and dress, and also to undress, tear down, strike, and dispose of safely and properly.

> I would take photos of the sets from pictures I worked on, because otherwise, the stuff would disappear!
>
> The work done for a film belongs to the film—it disappears; just doesn't exist anymore … a lot of it disintegrates. It (set research & records) wouldn't exist if I hadn't photographed them.
>
> —Norm Newberry (*Polar Express, The Mask, Avatar, The River, Ghost Story*)

It is always faster and easier to take away than to build, so *be mindful of the WAY you leave your locations after a shoot!*

The way that you leave any location will lead to your reputation throughout the industry.

Even if you have been filming in a restaurant or bar in a remote city, *your reputation follows you and your shooting company*.

In fact, it *leaves behind an impression forever* regarding the unique experience of allowing *any filming* to take place on the premises, *ever!*

Leaving a location with whatever improvements possible, as a 'thank you' to the owner for allowing filming, helps smooth the way for the next company that may want to film in that location. 'Pay it forward', in other words.

This becomes not only YOUR reputation, but that of the *entire film community*!

Reputation

You want to build a reputation of excellence and professionalism.

So much of what happens in the movie industry often happens quickly, with a phone call and a promise-**your word becomes your bond,** literally.

There is only one way to build this reputation; it is by keeping your word.

No matter what happens, your integrity is on the line, and you need to take this part of the job seriously.

We all know how hard it is to build trust; it only takes an instant to destroy it. Decide to be a TRUSTWORTHY Production Designer, and you will be welcomed into places others may not go. Building personal relationships goes far beyond your Art Department; you never know when you may need a farmer's barn or an old tractor for a shoot, and the only person the farmer will deal with is YOU, because of your personal friendship.

When the unexpected happens, the way to handle changes of any sort is by *respecting others' time and efforts through accurate communication; let them know personally there may be a delay, or even a cancellation.*

This is diplomacy and consideration. If you treat others, *especially strangers on a location,* with the courtesy and the respect that YOU would like to receive, you will quickly build a reputation as honourable, trustworthy, and reliable.

This means following-up, delivering contracts and payments on time, and whenever possible, **over-delivering on your promises!**

What does over-delivering mean, when shooting on location?

It could mean:

- Leaving the location in BETTER condition that you found it
- Cleaning MORE than the area used for filming
- Repair/replacing something small, yet memorable for the owner (i.e. a scratch on the bar surface that your painter could fix)
- Leaving a can of the paint colour used to repaint a room
- Replacing apartment numbers, to match those used in the shoot
- Fixing a broken step/doorknob/lock, etc.
- Planting flowers (and leaving them after the shoot).

These ways of over-delivering speak volumes about you and about your filming company!

Word-of-mouth travels far and wide; be certain it is POSITIVE about you and the filming company, and your reputation will be assured.

Wrap/archiving (books with samples and all records of paint finishes, etc.)

A true mark of over-delivering, and of the professional Production Designer, is found in the way they wrap out a project.

Some leave an empty office, clean, but with *no thought of future needs* or requirements, such as, *inserts, re-shoots, even a sequel or a next season!*

Again, putting yourself in someone else's place, such as the Production Designer who may follow you (it happens), ask yourself: what would you need to re-create that set?

Then, compile a binder with all of that information. As a courtesy. As a backup. As an aid to the next one in line who may need the information … which may even be YOU!

This is the best time to do so, because you already have nearly everything you need at your fingertips. Instead of throwing everything away, ***archive*** your project professionally. It may come in handy, and the process is a good practice to develop.

Figure 16.1 Layout board protecting floors

Included in the binder would be:

- List of sets and locations
- Plans for sets and directors' plans, including plot plans for locations (in scale)
- Paint colours, wallpapers, speciality trims, mouldings, architectural pieces (back bar, windows, stairs)
- Photos of key set dressing and sources
- Any backings noted, with instructions how to locate
- Speciality props, miniatures, breakaways, flags, etc.
- Notes for greens, nursery source, flowers, trees, shrubs, rocks, garden trellis, etc.
- List of signs, graphics, logos, neon, military badges, etc.
- Any speciality vehicles and signage
- Reduced copies of storyboards and set sketches
- Current script.

One successful Production Designer, **Tom Duffield**, has developed the habit of *gifting his directors* with a bound copy of the script for each movie; a 'quick-look' archive of each show, as a thank you. These are embossed with the director's name, and contain all of the above and more.

He also makes one for himself, and he now has a record of every project he's worked on, complete with resources to support any future questions or concerns.

As head of the Art Department, he also thanks the construction crews and the Art Department team for their help in making the film go so well with some type of show gifts to say 'thank you' and 'let's do it again sometime'.

His personal bookshelf of movie archive binders includes *Beetlejuice*, *The Birdcage*, *Ed Wood*, *Lone Survivor*, *Hell or High Water*, and *Patriots Day*, to name just a few.

Figure 16.2 Production Designer Tom Duffield's bookshelf of movie archive binders

CHAPTER 17

Networking and Business Package

Everyone you know, knows at least 10 people—each of these people are in a position to hire you, to recommend you, or to refer you for a position.

—Anonymous

Networking is simply cultivating good relationships.

We all want the same things; respect, consideration, good manners, honesty.

Nearly every Production Designer interviewed here, when asked the question, 'What do you look for in a potential new member of your team?' gave the same answer: '**_PEOPLE SKILLS. GET ALONG WITH THE TEAM. RELIABILITY_**.'

These qualities were more important than particular skills to getting hired!

One Production Designer explained; '_skills can be taught; personality cannot_'.

Professional Networking

As a Designer, you are **always** on a job interview! Your style is your brand. The way you present yourself communicates who you are as a Designer.

Honour this.

You will be recognized, noticed, and appreciated for your style. This translates into referrals and job offers, so be certain that your appearance truly reflects who you are as a Designer. Find your unique voice and mode of expression, and always bring your best to every decision you make.

We have learned that the set supports the character. _What type of character are you? Who do you want to be?_ Your answers may not always be the same, but if you have the courage to be **authentic**, you will always come across as genuine. This is how we develop personal style. (In the beginning, before you are sure of yourself, it's good policy to emulate the best. Someone you admire. Try not to copy.)

Always stand for **quality** in your own work and in your Art Department. When presenting your work, **only show your best**. It's better to show three of your best designs than four designs including one that's not so good. Go for quality over quantity.

Never feel that you need to include a greater number of pieces in your portfolio to demonstrate your experience! Present only your best. **_Employers tend to remember the worst piece_ you include**; if you know it's not your best, eliminate it. 'When in doubt, leave it out'.

Remember to include samples that reflect your personality; have fun with it!

> The whole business is based on *relationships*.
>   People have to like you in order to spend 12–15 hours per day with you under stressful conditions.
>   They have to TRUST you.
>
> Chuck Parker, Executive Director, ADG (TV Series, *Monk*)

Production Designers must embrace all of the arts: drawing, painting, architecture, writing, music, dance, theatre, and so on. Staying up to date with the arts keeps you aware of the cultural zeitgeist of the moment. As a Designer for a motion picture or television, you could be called on to design in any field imaginable, and you never know where inspiration will come from. For example, you might get an idea for designing a room by listening to a new song.

It isn't enough to simply draw, draft, and paint. You need to find what inspires you.

Figure 17.1 *North by Northwest* (1959). Academy Award-winning Production Designer Robert Boyle was inspired by his love of barns to create the stone cantilevered house in *North by Northwest*. Note the rustic appearance of the house, which is made of stone and weathered beams.

Figure 17.2 Cantilevered barn

Figure 17.3 Knee-brace detail

Building Your Reputation

Designers are typically selected when their style and skills match the style needed for the project. Be aware of your own style and the reputation you are building. You will be hired or referred for positions based on your previous work.

This is where style becomes extremely important. For example, someone proficient in spaceship design would be a natural choice for a science-fiction film. Additionally, there are Designers who will refuse to work on period pieces and choose to work on contemporary projects only. Be aware of the reputation you're building for yourself. Do you want to become an expert in one area or be proficient in a broad array of styles?

The way that you approach even the smallest job speaks volumes about you. Decide to be a professional! You will be respected and taken seriously, and the job offers you receive will reflect this.

- Take every opportunity to show your skills in Graphics and Design. You never know who will see your work or when a simple design you did as a favour will be noticed by someone with the power to hire you for another job.
- Learn as much as you can about the other departments you collaborate with. Your skills and positive attitude will be noticed, and your next job may be the result of a referral from a completely different department.
- Decide to be one of the best and do all you can do to utilize your talents to help others. The work offers will come to you through word-of-mouth and referrals. These are the best types of referrals, because they are already vetted (coming from trusted colleagues).

We have discussed how important visual representation is and how powerfully it communicates. Read the script carefully and glean your design parameters from there. Ensure that you are communicating with the Director regularly to define and refine the parameters through appropriate design choices.

Finding and selecting what is appropriate is essential to good Production Design.

This principle applies to your personal brand as well. For example, your business card is much more than a piece of paper with contact information.

It is a powerful statement of your style, brand, and the field you've chosen to work in.

Make sure it is appropriate to your brand and the work you do. Moreover, make sure you *love* your own business card. When you love your card, you will have pride in it and will enjoy handing it out.

You need to build a positive reputation, and the way to do that is:

- Never settle
- Insist on quality
- Push your boundaries (grow)
- Stay excited
- Be positive
- Bring energy to your work
- Collaborate.

Make up your mind to be the best Designer you can be. That will inform every decision you make, and your network of contacts and professionals will grow successfully.

People who bring their A game every day and are contributing to the project in every possible way will <u>always</u> be noticed and stand apart.

Excellence is the norm, which is why the industry is so hard to break into EXCELLENCE. Which means <u>your best</u>.

<u>NOT</u> to be confused with *perfectionism*; which is paralysis and simply not possible.

Just strive to do your best as a habit and you will be fine.

Production Design is not easy and is not for everyone. It can be incredibly rewarding and character building, and it provides unique opportunities for teamwork and collaboration. You might have the opportunity to work with 'A-list' talent, at the top of their game. ***These colleagues will add to your list of connections and multiply the power of your referrals***.

You may reunite with some of these colleagues on another project, or maybe you won't. You could see less experienced workers promoted or invited on to future projects while you are left behind; *do not take it personally!* Things can change at any moment, and often do; remain ready and prepared for your next job and accept it gracefully when it is offered.

Remember that due to the accelerated pace of film and television work, <u>you have the opportunity to grow rapidly as a Designer</u>. This is due to the fact that one week you may design a police station, and the next week, you may design a church wedding. <u>You will be required to design quickly</u>.

A career in the Art Department, whether as a Production Designer, Art Director, or something else, will teach you about more than just how to work on a film. These lessons are as valuable for your daily life as they are for securing a job:

- Do your best
- Be considerate
- Never gossip
- Always be on time and on budget
- Have a sense of humour
- Be flexible
- Never complain
- Be positive
- Smile, and have fun!

Qualities of a Successful Production Designer

In reviewing your work to create your digital portfolio, you should see growth, maturity, and confidence.

One of the goals of this book is to empower you with the knowledge needed to work as a Production Designer and an understanding of the qualities and skills required.

These include: *initiative, thoroughness, responsibility, flexibility, resourcefulness, consideration, dependability, reliability, responsibility, honesty, trustworthiness, adaptability, and being easy to get along with*.

It's a long list, but with some work you can embody them all and build a career in Production Design. A career as a Production Designer is like no other. If it is your passion, the rewards and fulfilment far outweigh the long hours and dedication necessary.

A career in filmmaking will prepare you for any job or work experience. The standards in filmmaking are so high, and the competition for jobs is so fierce, that only the best and the brightest succeed. The emphasis on quality, performance, integrity, and responsibility is also great preparation for **life itself**. You will always be dealing with people who are at the top of their game (who excel at what they do). This inspires us and challenges us to 'raise our own game' and continue to grow.

A **thirst for knowledge** and an active interest in nearly every aspect of life (especially the arts) can be some of the best qualities of a good Production Designer. Sometimes, these qualities even outweigh art skills and/or previous experience. **Never underestimate the power of enthusiasm, positive energy, and sincere interest! Always bring a smile**.

Production Design is different for every Designer, each has their own way of doing it, and no one does it exactly the same as another Designer. That's what makes Production Design so great!

A story is told of one set decorator who, just before it was time to bring the Director onto the set, made freshly popped popcorn. The decorator **knew** that the smell would make the set feel like a real home, and would trigger an **emotional** response to the set.

Showing your creativity through **all five** senses is a wonderful way to build your reputation. Imagine that you are pitching to a team who has seen it all. Stand out! Be unique! Most of all, be **proud** of everything you do. If you are diligent about creating a benchmark of designs and other work that you are proud of, you will find success.

Good luck with your portfolio, and remember, you are pitching **YOURSELF**. Make it count, make it memorable, and make it interesting!

Professional Business Package (Part 1)

Business Intro

Imagine you are presenting to a Producer or Director who may hire you for your dream job. Does your work reflect your style? Is it a true representation of your professionalism and standards?

Ask yourself:

- Does my work communicate the **basics**: neatness, clarity, organization?
- Does my work convey a sense of **style** or uniqueness that stands out from the crowd?
- Is my work **impeccable** (no misspelled words, grammatical errors, or sloppiness)?

- Does my work exhibit **QUALITY** and attention to detail?
- Does my work appear **thorough**, **clear**, and **interesting**?
- Does my work **pique the interest** and make viewers want to see more?

These are the things Producers and Directors look for when hiring someone new for their team. Of course, they are also looking for candidates with **passion** and genuine **sincerity**. This is a tall order, but it is also why Production Design isn't for everyone. Remember, you will be working with 'the best of the best', which means **you** must excel, too!

A business package includes:

- Short biography
- Résumé
- Cover letter
- Business card
- A simple website (separate from social media).

By now, you should have enough examples of your work to show your **proficiency** and your unique, clear style. The execution of your work gives an indication of how you will perform tasks (jobs) in real-world situations.

Your portfolio (including **business package**), will be evaluated on **presentation, quality, and variety of skills.**

Professional Business Package (Part 2)

Résumé

Your professional business package should reflect *who you are in style and tone*.

This means choosing a **type font** with great care, and if and when appropriate, adding colour according to your personal palette.

The goal of a résumé is to show focus and to list your most polished and professional work experience. You should strive to **edit** your information extremely well on your résumé so that it reflects only your best work—nothing more. It is better to have a short, streamlined résumé that fits on one page and focuses on the job you want than to have a long, rambling résumé listing every job you've ever had.

Every job entails some **leadership, responsibilities, and skills**.

List these in a positive, simple, and straightforward way. It is a mistake to try to embellish or 'pad' your work experience. Those who are hiring you are aware that you are a student just starting out or beginning a new career. Showing strength and confidence in presenting yourself in the best possible light will work in your favour. Clarity counts!

On your résumé, be sure to include:

- **Contact information:** be certain your information is clear and current
- **Education:** dates are optional
- **Work experience:** include your *top three experiences*

- **References:** offer to supply them
- **Special skills and talents:** these will set you apart; list all computer and tech skills, hobbies (such as photography), awards, languages, travel, professional memberships, etc.

Professional Business Package (Part 3)

Biography

Your biography should be short and concise. The purpose is to **briefly introduce yourself.**

Simply give a few positive descriptive facts about yourself. You're not selling here, just listing strong points. If you want to, you can also mention your future goals, clearly and honestly.

It's important for your biography to read as authentic, upbeat, and sincere. Try to strike a tone of sincerely presenting yourself without sounding arrogant or timid. This should not be the story of your life, and it is not the place to discuss family situations. Only the pertinent information that a future employer would want to see applies. A half page is sufficient.

Do not list any negatives! Stay positive and imagine someone is describing you in a short introduction to a crowd of strangers. This will help you keep the facts impersonal yet interesting. The idea is to spark the audience's attention so that they are intrigued and want to know more about you.

Professional Business Package (Part 4)

Cover Letter

Use a cover letter for every position you apply for. It should be personalized and tailored to fit each company and individual that you contact.

Take the time to research the company, job, or position you are applying for, and try to find the **name** of the person to whom you will be sending your application. *This is good business*, and will set you apart from hundreds of generic applicants.

The mention of one of the company's projects you admire or some award or charity they support shows the employer that you have 'done your homework' (i.e. researched thoroughly) and are serious about working there. You will impress them before they have even met you!

Use a template for this cover letter. There are many samples available online, in many different styles. Choose one that follows professional business letter guidelines; your letter will be read by the business end of the department or company first. If your letter doesn't pass this first standard test (due to sloppiness, spelling errors, incorrect letter structure, etc.) it probably will NOT make it to the next level.

Keep this letter short and professional; it should easily fit on one page. Greet the contact person, mention the position you are applying for, and state that your résumé and short bio are included with the letter.

After a statement or two about the company and why you would like to work there, *offer to follow the letter with a phone call in a week or two.*

This is important! Most applicants use the standard phrase 'feel free to contact me anytime', which puts the emphasis on THEM to find and contact you.

By offering to follow up yourself, **you are making it easy for them to contact you again** AND **you are showing initiative and responsibility**. This will be noticed and appreciated.

There is a saying: **'Never turn down a meeting'**. This means that you should *take every chance you get to have a face-to-face meeting*, even if it is not for the position you are interested in. The goal is to make connections. Everyone you meet has the power to refer or to recommend you.

Also, a meeting is the perfect opportunity to learn what the company is looking for in their employees and to find out what you would have to do in order to be hired by the company.

Professional Business Package (Part 5)

Business Cards

Your business card needs to say **who you are as a professional** and do so in a way that communicates your **style, taste, and individuality**.

The worst mistake you can make as a Designer is to use cheap card stock.

Quality is instantly recognized and appreciated, and so is a lack of quality.

Good design can be done inexpensively and creatively using a variety of type fonts, colours, and even images, but *nothing can save a flimsy, cheap piece of paper*.

A hastily printed, standard-issue, inexpensive business card screams 'I don't care about quality or details!'

This is definitely **not** the impression you are aiming for!

Business cards don't have to cost a fortune, but they do have to be **the best you can afford**. A business card can be so beautiful, so interesting, and so memorable that people will actually keep and save your card; it becomes a connection to you. Everyone in the business has saved a card they like just because there was something special about it. For this reason, and because this is a **design field**, you will want to invest in the best quality card stock you can afford to have your information printed on.

Select your type fonts and colours with extreme care, paying special attention to the design and layout of your personal card. **This will represent you**; it is like a *mini-portfolio of your work and your style*.

Aim for **quality, style, simplicity, and individuality**.

This is one of the most important design statements you will make; it is NOT the time to compromise by using anything sub-standard.

Make sure that your business card design is the best you can do, and that it is something you can be proud to pass out. People will respond to that energy.

The example here shows the evolution of design for a business card:

- Image 1 was the first pass: generic, and with a basic font
- Image 2 shows more thoughtful attention to detail: the blueprint/title block style and drafting font
- Image 3 is personal, simple, and a much better layout: the subject used his own signature!

The final result is one that is interesting, clear, appropriate and memorable. Home run!

Figure 17.4 Business card design (evolution)

Figure 18.1 Library of the Academy of Motion Picture Arts and Sciences/Margaret Herrick Library

CHAPTER 18

Resources

The human management part of the job … is not easy, many are not good at it, some do not like it.

—Norm Newberry (*The Best Little Whorehouse in Texas, Polar Express, The River*)

ADG
Address: 11969 Ventura Blvd, Studio City, CA 91604
Phone: (818) 762-9995

ACADEMY/Margaret Herrick Library
Address: 333 S La Cienega Blvd, Beverly Hills, CA 90211
Phone:(310) 247-3020

Museum of Television/Paley Center
Address: 465 N Beverly Dr, Beverly Hills, CA 90210
Phone:(310) 786-1000

These are not meant to be endorsements, but suggested resources

Debbies Book – Prop Houses Category Search
thesourcebookonline.com/search.php?by_search=category&search=Prop+Houses

Vinyl signs & banners
Address: 5554 Sepulveda Blvd, Culver City, CA 90230
Phone: (310) 390-8104

Neon
nightsofneon.com/
rentneon.com/catalog (Heaven or Las Vegas neon sign/prop rentals)

Nurseries/Greens & Garden

Jackson Shrub
Address: 11505 Vanowen St, North Hollywood, CA 91605
Phone: (818) 982-0100

Greenset
www.greenset.com/
11617 Dehougne St
(818) 764-1231

Backings

www.jcbackings.com/

Picture Vehicles

cinemavehicles.com/
picturecarwarehouse.net/

Prop Houses/Rentals

www.omegacinemaprops.com/
hpr.com/

Furniture Rentals/Office Equipment

www.productionhub.com/directory/.../props-furniture-household-accessories
www.omegacinemaprops.com/
www.theacme.com/

Art Supplies

www.cartersexton.com/

Locations/Warehouses

www.rtrlocations.com/
variety411.com/us/los-angeles/location-services-equipment/

Legal/Clearances

www.researchhouse.ca/services/

Paint Supplies

www.markspaint.com

Cleaning Crews

office-cleaning.eden.io/janitorial/service

Flower Supply

originallaflowermarket.com

PLUS ALL OF THE USUAL SUSPECTS: Smart & Final, Staples, Office Depot, etc.

CHAPTER 19

Credits

PASSION is essential! It's about light & shade and how the objects capture light and create shadow … look at Film Noir! It doesn't have to cost a fortune.
—Jim Bissell (*Monuments Men, Mission Impossible*)

Interviews/Quotes

Tom Duffield
Lone Survivor, Patriots Day, Hell or High Water, Ed Wood

Norm Newberry
Ghost Story, Polar Express, The Mask, The River, Avatar

Peter Wooley (BLAZING SADDLES, HIGH ANXIETY, THE DAY AFTER)

Ward Preston (AIRPLANE, TOWERING INFERNO, POSEIDON ADVENTURE)

Henry Bumstead (TO KILL A MOCKINGBIRD, THE STING, VERTIGO)

Bill Ross (COLUMBO, MISSION IMPOSSIBLE-TV, BRADY BUNCH)

John Corso (COALMINER'S DAUGHTER, BREAKFAST CLUB, PRETTY IN PINK)

Rick Carter (STAR WARS, LINCOLN, FORREST GUMP, AVATAR)

Jim Bissell (ET, MISSION IMPOSSIBLE—ROGUE NATION, MONUMENTS MEN, GOOD NIGHT, AND GOOD LUCK)

Jeannine Oppewal (LA CONFIDENTIAL, PLEASANTVILLE, CATCH ME IF YOU CAN, SEABISCUIT)

Wynn Thomas (HIDDEN FIGURES, A BEAUTIFUL MIND, INSIDE MAN, DO THE RIGHT THING)

Nelson Coates – PRESIDENT, ART DIRECTORS GUILD, LOCAL #800 (RUNAWAY JURY, 50 SHADES DARKER, FLIGHT, KISS THE GIRLS, MURDER AT 1600)

Chuck Parker – EXECUTIVE DIRECTOR, ART DIRECTORS GUILD (MONK, 90210)

Kenn Ferro, DIRECTOR, SCHOOL OF MOTION PICTURES, AAU SAN FRANCISCO, CA

Lee Redmond, DIRECTOR, CINEMATOGRAPHER

Quotes from Transcripts: (1981)

Bob Boyle (NORTH BY NORTHWEST, CAPE FEAR, THOMAS CROWN AFFAIR, THE BIRDS, GAILY, GAILY)

John DeCuir, Sr (CLEOPATRA, HELLO DOLLY, THE KING AND I)

Ted Haworth (STRANGERS ON A TRAIN, SOME LIKE IT HOT, LONGEST DAY, MARTY)

Harold Michelson (STAR TREK: THE MOTION PICTURE, HISTORY OF THE WORLD, PT.1)

Albert Brenner (PRETTY WOMAN, BULLITT, BACKDRAFT)

Dick Sylbert (THE GRADUATE, BABY DOLL, CHINATOWN, ROSEMARY'S BABY, DICK TRACY)

Gene Allen (MY FAIR LADY, A STAR IS BORN, CHEYENNE SOCIAL CLUB)

Special Thanks

Tom Duffield	Henry Bumstead
Norm Newberry	Bill Ross
Kenn Ferro	Ward Preston
Lee Redmond	John Corso
Bill Major	

ADG

Laura Kamagowa

Rosemarie Knopka

Michael Baugh/Perspectives Editor and Photos

Art Directors Guild, International Alliance of Theatrical Stage Employees (IATSE) Local #800

Nelson Coates – PRESIDENT, ADG LOCAL #800

Chuck Parker – EXECUTIVE DIRECTOR, ART DIRECTORS GUILD, LOCAL #800 (MONK)

Acknowledgment

This book is meant to honour all early Production Designers and to empower anyone interested in the world of Production Design.

—*Peg McClellan*

CHAPTER 20

To Read

We are not thinking of films in terms of sets.
 We're thinking of the overall, the whole film, and I think it's our RESPONSIBILITY to see that that direction is carried forward.
—Bob Boyle (*North by Northwest, Cape Fear, Thomas Crown Affair, The Birds, Gaily, Gaily*)

Sleepless in Hollywood by Linda Obst

Hello, He Lied by Linda Obst

What An Art Director Does by Ward Preston

What! And Give Up Show Business? by Peter Wooley

Designing Films; Portrait of a Hollywood Artist by Richard (Dick) Sylbert

Film Directing Shot by Shot by Steven Katz

The Mailroom by David Rensin

The Art of the Hollywood Backdrop by Richard Isackes and Karen Maness

Caligari's Cabinet and Other Grand Illusions by Donald Albrecht

Film Architecture by Dietrich Neumann

Henry Bumstead and the World of Hollywood Art Direction

Special Thanks

This book is dedicated to all Production Designers and Art Directors who came before; and to their excellent examples of leadership, collaboration, and professionalism.

My special thanks go to:

Ken Ferro—for recommending me to write this book (and also for his interview).

Lee Redmond—for his support on every level (and also for his interview).

Norm Newberry—for sharing his home office, original sketches & photos, and for his contribution to the Special Effects chapter (and also for his interview plus peer review).

Michael Baugh—for tirelessly providing photos and captions from the ADG *Perspectives* magazine, as editor-in-chief.

Tom Duffield (my first interview!)—for his generosity and time, access to behind-the-scenes materials, tech support, peer review, assistance with cover design, and unlimited support for this project at all times (and also for his interview).

The Art Directors Guild: Laura Kamagawa, Rosemarie Knopka, Nelson Coates, Chuck Parker—for their total support of the book in every way possible (and also their interviews).

And the Academy Library: Howard Prouty and **Ann Coco**—for their encouragement and full support (and permission to use the Academy Library image in Chapter 18).

The Menzies Family Collection—courtesy of Pamela Lauesen

Sarah Pickles—my talented Editor who brought this book to the finish line with cheerful dedication and support.

Index